M000013624

On Kitten Creek

On Kitten Creek

SEARCHING FOR THE SACRED

Nancy Swihart

CLADACH
Publishing

Copyright © 2017
by Nancy Swihart
Published by:
Cladach Publishing
PO Box 336144
Greeley, CO 80633
http://cladach.com

All rights reserved.

Scripture quotations are taken from the *New American Standard Bible*® (NASB), Copyright © 1960, 1962, 1963, 1968, 1971, 1972, 1973, 1975,1977, 1995 by The Lockman Foundation. Used by permission. www.Lockman.org

ISBN-13: 978-1-945099-02-1
ISBN-10: 1-945099-02-X
Library of Congress Catalog Number: 2017941439

Printed in the U.S.A.

To my husband, Judd~
whose energy and people skills were the glue
that held our vision together;

and

To our three children, Derrick, Dan, and Sara~
who never complained about our choice of living
styles but gladly joined the adventure.

CONTENTS

PREFACE

Dinner is over. Grandchildren hold their breath as the candles on the cake are lit and the birthday song is finally sung. No one cares how many candles are on the cake, for now we are all looking at the presents piled on the side table. Elsie, the blonde, blue-eyed ten-year-old is chosen to bring the gifts, one by one, and place them on Opa's lap. Some shiny rocks, a lopsided John Deere tractor drawn on construction paper, work gloves, much-needed tools: each gift represents love and thoughtfulness. With his opened gifts sitting before him on the table, my husband, Judd, leans back and beams at his family. He is loved!

Gift-receiving is a great analogy for our lives. The hundred-and-sixty-acre farm on Kitten Creek Road, which creates a back-drop for our story, has become a vibrant community of family and friends. Many, many people have contributed to the fabric of our lives and, as a result, have been a testimony of God's presence and his involvement in our otherwise mundane existence.

With this farm have come many layers of wrapped gifts given by God, who loves to inhabit our space along with us—mystery in the midst of the mundane. This book is based on the adventures of unwrapping those presents, the contents of which we never could have guessed by shaking the package: the gift of community; the gift of sorrows and celebrations; the gift of land

and buildings; even the gift of the animals that eventually filled the farm. You will find these gifts hidden in the context of our lives, just as we found them.

As we attempt to live a sacramental life, we are given opportunities to unwrap—in our clumsy and fumbling ways—God's presence in our daily, otherwise earthbound, lives. In those moments of willingly accepting and unwrapping those gifts, we find ourselves living a sacred existence.

INTRODUCTION
Mystery in the Midst of the Mundane

"The world is crying out for lived stories and a passionately viable present. Lived and lasting change born of deep connections, whole-person sinewing—mind, spirit, emotions, body—with the Incarnate One who invades our histories and has eternally raised the bar for human interaction."
–Sally Morgenthaler

ARE YOU HUNGRY FOR A LIFE that is more than simple existence, for something to give you hope, for surprises bathed in an eternal aura? Do you long for fellow travelers, for genuine community, a place where you can tell your story and listen to others?

I, also, have yearned to know that there is more to life than looking for the latest fashion, finding new recipes and decorating tips, or engaging in conversations that never get to the nitty-gritty of life. I have needed to go deeper, to become better acquainted with my Creator, to ponder his character and my responses to him, to look for the sacred in my daily life, and to find others to join me on that journey.

As a young mother in Southern California, I found myself "homesick" for God. Life was good; no traumas had interrupted my daily existence. My husband, the director of a Christian counseling center, and I had three small children, I led a ladies' Bible study, and I had great friends. But I longed for something more—a life invaded by the Holy One. I needed to see God in my daily existence.

My greatest Christian mentors have been authors, theologians, philosophers, missionaries; and Francis and Edith Schaeffer wore all of those hats. After reading Edith Schaeffer's *L'Abri*, the story of how God used their family in the Alps of Switzerland, my heart longed for an adventure that could come from working and walking by faith with the Creator of the Universe in a day-by-day experience. I found myself captured by a desire to be part of a community that could formulate biblical ways of living and responding to the world in which we had been placed.

Why did the story of L'Abri tug at my heart? The last statement in Edith's introduction summed it up for me: They desired to show the "reality of the fact that God exists, and that he is the One who has, time after time, answered prayer in the midst of well-nigh impossible circumstances to bring about something out of nothing." The practical kind of life I desired was one where this "something out of nothing" God was answering prayer and walking with us through our day-to-day circumstances. I yearned to offer a home like L'Abri where life happened in the context of God's shelter and his direction, where we lived out the truth of *The God Who Is There*, and who *Is Not Silent* (as the titles of Francis's seminal books declare).

My story is written in the following pages, the story of how I found God's surprising interceptions when I looked for him. Did our ministry grow to be exactly like L'Abri? No. God has taken our gifts—Judd's and mine—which are not those of Edith and Francis, and has written the story he had in mind. Most of the story unfolds in a tiny town in Kansas on a run-down old farm. This scene was not the vision I would have pictured when the desire took root in my heart back in sunny California. "Kansas!" I had almost sneered when Judd announced that he had an interview for a job in Manhattan, Kansas. I imagined flat wheat fields and empty spaces. How did God change my ridicule into joy and anticipation? That is part of the story.

I am writing now from the perspective of a woman who is a grandmother of eleven grandchildren (the twelfth is in heaven). I can see more clearly today than thirty-some years ago when I thought I knew how walking with God as a family would look. *Of course,* I thought, *it will look at least something like the L'Abri story.* I had lots to learn. My expectations, my wish dreams, my visions had to be set aside many times. That was part of the journey.

I thought God would give us a large home on a few acres. Instead, God gave us an old cottage with no indoor toilet, no running water (but an elegant outhouse), a big old barn, and lots of outbuildings on one hundred and sixty acres.

I thought I would be the omnipresent hostess with young people coming to live with us, study with us, and go out and change the world. Instead, this tiny cottage had no room for hosting those guests, nor could I be the hostess who welcomed guests daily, because I needed to work to help support the family.

When I taught at Manhattan Christian College, I would take the back steps up to my office. At the top of the stairs, as I opened the door to the faculty commons, my eyes fell on a sign sitting prominently on the desk of one of our teaching assistants. "Life is what happens while you are busy making other plans." It was a silent and frequent reminder to me. Often, while I was busy trying to make sure that something would happen, I would look over my shoulder and see God doing something entirely different—and always better.

As an idealist, I sometimes get caught up in a wish-dream; but God may have other plans. I have learned that whenever God rejects one of our dreams, it is not out of his disdain for our wishes, but that he has something better. In denying my wish dreams, God did not hold back his blessings. He had a better plan!

Looking back, I can see God's plan painted in pictures that we could only uncover as we lived under his leadership. His plan was like the old paint-by-number pictures of my childhood. The pictures became beautiful only when I followed the numbers carefully, choosing the right colors to fill in the spaces until the image began to appear: a galloping horse, a cuddly puppy, or a lovely cabin by a stream. It took patience to see how the picture would finally look. The waiting can be difficult. Then when the work is finished we can step back and see how all those tiny little dabs and swaths became a distinct image with coherence and beauty.

In this book, I share how God patiently made something beautiful out of our mundane world. Often he had to redirect me, shepherd me, teach me and then pick me up when I fell. Living without many financial resources, building community, raising sheep, horses, cows and caring for animals, hosting thousands of people, are all part of the story. I invite you to walk the farm paths with me. You can join me in welcoming guests to a rain-drenched and muddy conference in the barn, search in the brush for the blind old sheep, and stand in the star-lit night as buses unload hundreds of guests to walk through a biblical account of Christ's life, death, and resurrection.

In becoming acquainted with this century-old farm and a simple lifestyle of living by faith, I trust you will be encouraged to take whatever it is that God has placed in your hand and let him write his story into it. I pray you will be encouraged in your faith journey to seek the hand of God in your everyday life and that God will give you glimpses of the picture he is painting through your life.

Section One

The Gifts of Place and People

1.
Kansas, Here We Come

WE LOADED THE LAST of our belongings, pulled the loading door down, and locked the U-Haul truck. Judd would maneuver this truck across the desert, over the mountains, and through the plains. The suitcases, dog, cat, and one of the children would be riding with me in the gold Torino station wagon.

Ready!

After tearful good-byes to family and church friends the night before, only a few neighbors and friends had gathered for our departure. Mrs. McIlwain, our elderly neighbor, was one of the first to show up and watch these final tasks. She had seen us through many stages of family life. This dear lady was there ten years before, watching us move with two toddlers into our newly-purchased home. The historian of the neighborhood, having lived her entire married life in the bungalow across the street, she told many interesting stories. She also freely dispensed advice on how to mow our yard, what plants grew best, when to plant, and when to water. Sharing recipes and encouraging me as a young mother showed me she loved me in her way.

Prickly on the outside, soft on the inside, Mrs. McIlwain tried to stay matter-of-fact as tears filled her blue eyes and choked her voice. "Now, you write to me and let me know how you are. I promise to watch the house for you until the new owner gets here." I hugged her soft, warm body and planted a quick kiss on her square, wrinkled jaw. She would keep her promise! She had been my watch-dog, my compass, and sometimes my irritant; but I loved that old woman, and I knew that she loved our family as if we were her own.

So much living had gone on in this green ranch-style home on the corner of Oakdale Drive and Community Street. Here our family had grown from two adults and two toddlers to two adults and three active, elementary-aged children. Lots of love, lots of tears, lots of growing.

One concern hovered in the back of our minds as we filled the car with suitcases. All the pieces for the move had lined up, except one important part. The year before, when Judd told the Shepherd's House board that we were sensing that God was directing us elsewhere, they had asked him to give them one more year. In that year, Judd had helped to set the stage for a new director and had also received an offer from Kansas State University to teach in Family Studies. Our California house had sold at the last minute, which was also a miraculous answer to prayer, and we were looking forward to eventually buying our dream home in Kansas, which Judd and I had found on our trip to Manhattan for his interview.

By now we had sorted, packed, and loaded our belongings. We had committed. We were going. But questions loomed. We had no rental home to move into when we arrived. What would we do? Where would we sleep? And what about the animals?

Sharon, our good friend in Manhattan, had faithfully been looking for a rental home big enough for a family with three children, that would also allow pets. One of our last tasks before we loaded into the truck and station wagon was to find out where we would live when we got to Manhattan. Judd called Sharon one more time: "Have you found anything yet?" His voice betrayed his anxiety.

"No," she confessed. But always an optimist, she continued, "I am going out today, and I'm sure I'll find something!" Faith moves forward, and so we did.

Eleven-year-old Derrick and ten-year-old Dan were eager to be off on their new adventure despite some misgivings. They would miss the only home they could remember and the friendships forged in this little community, but they were ready for adventure, and the thought of riding in a big truck with Dad propelled them. Sara, at just-turned-six, was happy to go anywhere her family went.

Judd pulled away from the curb, the boys waving to the McIlwains and several others who had joined them to say goodbye. I backed out of the drive and followed the truck down Oakdale toward Roscoe Blvd. We were off!

Before the house was out of sight, Sara turned and looked back at the only home she had ever known, her voice filled with concern. "Poor Goldie! Do you think Munga will remember to pick him up?" My mother, who would remain in California with my brother's family, had agreed to care for Goldie. Mom loved cats, especially yellow cats. However, Goldie, our old yellow cat, was still in the backyard waiting for someone to take him to my mother's home. Unfinished business. Goldie had found us nine years before and had allowed my toddlers to drag him around, loving every minute of their attention.

Sara's brown eyes brimmed with tears. I tried to reassure her. "Munga loves Goldie. He'll be happy with her," but a lump formed in my throat at the thought of leaving him behind. Munga would now become his guardian.

But Sara was already looking forward at the U-Haul truck in front of us. "I can't wait till I get to ride with Daddy."

Home, grandmothers, cousins, and friends were difficult to leave, but our lives and destinies lay ahead of us now.

The protocol was set: Judd would lead the way in the large U-Haul with most of our earthly possessions. I would follow in the family station wagon. Fancy, the "chosen" cat, would be in his little blue carrier for the duration of the journey to Kansas. Berry, our young Doberman, was free to move around in the back of the station wagon beside the cat carrier. Our suitcases and coolers filled the back seat. The boys would ride shotgun in the truck with Dad, taking turns riding with me and allowing Sara sometimes to ride in the "big truck."

We headed out across the desert on a road we had often taken over the years, unaware this was the last trip we would ever make across that particular stretch. This adventure would determine the destinies of our lives.

What compelled us to take this journey? What excited us about this move to the center of the country? The desire for change had stirred in our hearts for over a year, one of the catalysts being Edith Schaeffer's *L'Abri*. We loved the thought of family doing ministry from their home. In Judd's ministry, directing Shepherd's House, a Christian counseling center in the San Fernando Valley, he served many hurting people. But the children and I had no part in that ministry.

After reading of the Schaeffer's daily experiences of God's faithfulness in Switzerland, I longed and prayed for a home our family could use where we would see God working in our everyday lives, bringing his presence and miracles into the mundane. I wanted my children to live with that expectation and to experience the joy of living a life that involved adventuring with God, though the form of that ministry had not yet taken shape.

It seemed to me the truck, station wagon, and their occupants moved across the western countryside in a cocoon of God's protection. From where did this sense of safety and destiny come?

The connections and friends we had made in California had been stimulating and fruitful. Judd had recently published a book on languages of love, *How Do You Say I Love You?* (Inter-Varsity Press), which was the first ever to be written on the subject. Yet here we were, going—by choice—to a rural, small, isolated town in the Midwest that few of our friends knew existed.

Those friends asked, "Have you given this thought, Judd?"

One friend, Gerry, had lunch with my husband, hoping to change his mind. "You know this is where things are happening, Judd. Southern California is alive with opportunities, vision, ideas. You are just getting started. Think of all you can accomplish out here. You would give this up to move to the prairies?" Gerry, previously the mayor of a thriving Southern California town, pastored a church he hoped to grow into a megachurch. He had co-authored a book with Judd and had vision and dreams of what they could do together.

Judd slowly set his cup down, leaned back in his chair, and smiled. In his mind, this topic was settled. "God is in Kansas, also, Gerry."

Our visit to Manhattan in April for Judd's interview had encouraged us—and impressed us with the small city nestled in the Flint Hills. This university town offered a stimulating and lively environment. On our last morning in Manhattan, we met the realtor that our friends had recommended. We had told her on the phone what we were desiring, and she had an idea.

When we drove up to the house, our jaws dropped. Were our eyes deceiving us? Situated just off the highway stood, what seemed to us, a fortress. A large, three-story stone house towered above the road, probably looking even bigger because of its position on the hill.

Compared to our ranch-style home in California, the house was a mansion. As we stepped out of the car, our hearts were racing. Before us stood our dream: a house with lots of space for guests, nine acres, an incredible stone barn, an old smokehouse and other stone outbuildings. The home had character and history. We entered it through the back door and stepped into, of all things, a beautiful country-blue kitchen with old walnut cupboards. I was exultant! Surely this was God's sign that the house would be ours. We took pictures, wandered through the house, the acres, and the barn. So much to tell our friends back in California who had been praying for us!

When we got back to California, of course, we shared the good news. I displayed pictures of "our" house to all of our friends. Yes, God was good! Even a blue kitchen! He was giving us our hearts' desire.

We had stayed in touch with the owners, who were themselves looking for a home in San Diego. At first, we tried a three-way sale, thinking that would be the best for us all. They were facing the high prices of California. Our home had quadrupled in price over the ten years that we had owned it, so our situation was the opposite of theirs. The three-way trade did not work. We sold our home, but they did not find a home. So there would be more negotiating after we arrived in Manhattan; but living in that house would be a dream come true.

Meanwhile, we depended on Sharon to find a rental for us.

By the time we got to Montrose, Colorado, we were ready for stretching, relaxing, and celebrating with family. Our children had spent many happy times with their cousins in California before Judd's brother's family, followed by his sister's family, and even his parents had all chosen to relocate to this beautiful part of the country. It was sibling and cousin reunion time, and a welcome oasis on the long, cross-country trek.

The next day, as the girls splashed in the plastic wading pool and the boys played daredevil on their bicycles, Judd excused himself to make another desperate call. We were two days out from our destination; would we have a place to land when we got to Manhattan?

"Sharon? It's Judd. Any news?"

"Oh, Judd," Sharon's voice was apologetic. "I thought I had the perfect place, but they won't take any animals. I promise I'll keep looking!

What could he say? It seemed as though we were standing at the edge of a precipice with no bridge across to the other side.

Faith rest. That was a phrase I had heard Judd use early in our marriage. And we had "faith-rested" getting the job, "faith-rested" selling our house, and now we were going to have to "faith-rest" this rental thing, also.

Early the next morning, after saying farewell to our dear extended family, we again headed our vehicles toward Kansas. We would have to cross the mountains before we reached the plains, and the truck was giving Judd trouble as we neared Monarch Pass. We had crawled over several passes. Altitude and steep inclines were taking a toll.

Monarch Summit loomed ahead when I noticed, through my rear-view mirror, that Judd had pulled over to the road's edge, a steep drop-off not far from the passenger door. My husband, my son, my daughter, and all our earthly possessions were in that truck; and to my eyes, that truck was in a very dangerous predicament—apparently dangling on the side of a steep incline.

My knuckles white on the car's steering wheel, I pulled into the Summit parking lot and stopped. This was before cell phones. I waited.

Ten-year-old Dan, our adventurous son, was riding shotgun with me at the time. While I sat and worried and prayed, Dan had his eye on the gondolas running up and down the slopes. "Oh, man, what fun! Don't you think we would have time to take a ride while Dad gets the truck fixed? We'd have time, wouldn't we?"

Anxiety or fun: choices. Judd had hiked up to the parking lot to find a mechanic, and on his way past the car, he had informed us that it was a probable vapor lock. A mechanic was going down and see what he could do.

I was relieved; they were going to be all right. Now Dan and I had nothing but time on our hands.

"Well, maybe we *can* forget the drama here and have some fun. Is it fair, though? What will your dad think?"

Dan looked at me with eagerness and pleading. Then, chucking everything to the wind, I gave in to Dan's pleas. Rather than be stuck in the parking lot waiting, the two of us dared to have an adventure of our own that day.

The ride up the mountain in a little box, dangling high above the trees, exhilarated us. Dan was enthralled, and somehow, I found that the enclosure eased my fear of heights. I relaxed and enjoyed the bird's-eye view. From our vantage point, we could see the truck in the distance, the traffic passing it slowly. What beauty lay below us, as our little cabin swayed its way up the mountainside. We could see up and down the range. In the distance, the other side of the mountain fell away; below us the sight of cedar forests and aspen groves. The tram took us along the crest that forms the Continental Divide to an observation building and deck at the top. From there we could see for miles.

In less than a half hour we were back. We found an impatient husband and father waiting for us.

Not finding me in my car when the truck finally reached the Monarch parking lot, Judd and the other two children waited in the gift shop. By the time Dan and I returned from our ride, Judd was ready to get back on the road. He had a difficult time understanding my frivolity and was not in the mood to take time out for the other two children to ride a little car up the mountain, when we had a long drive ahead of us. So, the difficult decision was made that we couldn't take any more travel time on this mountain pass. We had to keep moving forward.

Limon, Colorado, was the last overnight stop on our journey. Wheat harvesters had flooded this little town when we drove in. Not having much acquaintance with the harvesting milieu, we were educated that evening. Every hotel was full of men come to harvest Colorado wheat, working their way north as the crops ripened. No room in the inns. At the very edge of town, we discovered a run-down motel with a blinking, broken sign: "Va-ancy." Dim lighting revealed peeling paint and trash in the drive; but we needed a place to sleep.

The shabby room contained two double beds. The boys shared one of the beds; Judd and I shared the other; and between the two beds we spread blankets for Sara. I think the sheets were clean, but the mattress had issues. Judd and I discovered that the center of our bed sank about a foot lower than the sides. We tried to cling to the edge of each side to keep from smothering each other. Rest was scarce that night.

Bleary eyed the next morning, we loaded back into the vehicles. Judd found a way to call Sharon again before we left. No house, yet, and we would be in Manhattan by evening.

The scenery slowly changed from browns to shades of green. Long fields of yellow wheat gave way to rolling pastures dotted with Black Angus and red Herefords.

Our orange Tabby, Fancy, was all but voiceless by now. Not enjoying the close confinement in his carrier, he had incessantly verbalized his complaints across the desert. By the time we reached the mountains, he had minimized his loud comments to specific incidents. If we were quiet, he was quiet. If we talked, he tried to drown us out. So we had learned to commit ourselves to long periods of quiet, thoughtful travel. On the other hand, our young Doberman, Berry, seemed to have caught the Swihart family sense of adventure. She thoroughly enjoyed watching out the back window or curling up beside Fancy's carrier.

The sun was beginning its journey down into the western sky when we pulled off I-70 and headed down into the valley where Manhattan nestles among the Flint Hills. We were accustomed to California's dry scenery in July. The hills here were a verdant green, and the sky a deep azure blue.

When Derrick rode with me, he read aloud from James Herriot's, *All Things Bright and Beautiful.* His grey-flecked eyes twinkled and his face broke into a grin as he read, from the large paperback, the detailed word pictures Herriot painted of his beloved Yorkshire hills. We gazed out the car windows and chuckled at his descriptions of predicaments and escapades with the English country folk and their charming way of life.

In this way, Herriot's stories became the backdrop for my

perception of the Flint Hills of Kansas. Even now, when I look upon our hills, the ghosts of Herriot's stories linger in my mind.

Following Sharon's directions, we wound our way through town to the Reker home on a little side street. As we pulled up to the curb, George, Sharon and their three little boys came rushing out of the house. "Welcome! Welcome to Kansas!" they shouted from the steps. Although the boys had never known us, they absorbed their parent's enthusiasm. Judd would be working with George in the Family Studies Department at Kansas State.

Slowly we crawled out of our vehicles, stretched our legs and rubbed our backs. The question hung thick in the air. "Well? Have you found anything, yet?" Behind the question loomed a bigger one: "Are we homeless?"

But we found Sharon jubilant. She had gone out again that morning with the realtor, when something seemed to pop into the realtor's mind. "You know what! Our pastor just moved out of the parsonage on Church Street. No one is living there now; it's empty. I think they'd be willing to rent it. Maybe that would work for your friends."

The house was in a residential area, near a school, they would allow pets, and it was perfect! Our faith-rest had been faith-tested, and God was "there and not silent" as Francis Schaeffer would say.

That next morning, with the help of young Nat and Tim Bascom, friends of the Rekers and soon-to-be part of the core of our "ministry," we were unloading. By noon the truck was unloaded; by evening the beds were set up, linens unpacked, and we had begun to settle into life in Kansas.

2.
Readjusting Dreams

OUR CHURCH STREET RENTAL was an answer to our immediate prayer, but the bigger question was, when would we have a permanent home? When Judd and I had visited Manhattan for his interview, we had found the perfect property for sale, and we were in the midst of trying to settle a contract for it. While we negotiated, I planned.

One morning, soon after our move, I pulled out my graph paper and sat down at the dining-room table of our rental house. Convinced that the old stone house we had seen on our first trip to Manhattan, would be our new home, I set to planning. *Let's see, the old cupboard will fit well in the dining room,* I thought as I drew a little rectangle in the corner of the middle room. *Sara's bedroom will be at the top of the stairs, and the boys' will be across the hall.*

The children were busy with their activities, and I was preparing to "nest" in our new home. After all, it was exactly what a L'Abri kind of house should look like. And I had dreamed of a big house with a blue kitchen.

The house was still on the market. As we bargained, I was-confident and content to let God work out the details. We took the boys and Sara to see the house so they could imagine themselves living there. We walked through the house with the realtor, dreaming. On the third floor, which was a large, open space, we would put bunk beds for the guests who would come to stay awhile. The boys loved the barn, the underground cellar, the ice house. So much to explore and enjoy.

Sara was a little overwhelmed by the size of the house, especially when she wandered out to the backyard and got separated from us. By the time she found us, she was thinking that this may not be the house she wanted.

But, we'd have time to ease her fears as negotiations with the owners continued.

As time passed, the decision became a serious matter of prayer. We finally decided that we would offer forty-thousand dollars under the asking price. That was our fleece. If God wanted us to have the house, and I was sure he did, the owners would accept. We would take their response as God's sign.

Waiting was difficult; I filled the time by working on my graph paper. *The couch will go here, under the window, and the big comfortable chairs will go here, facing the couch.*

When the phone rang, I jumped up to answer it. Our realtor was on the line. She spoke with caution. "Nancy, they have come back with a significant counter offer. You may want to consider it."

My heart dropped. Judd and I had agreed that our offer was our final litmus test.

She continued, "I told them what you were planning to do with the house. They know about L'Abri. They came down thirty thousand, but they can't afford to go lower."

We had to refuse. I wish I could say thankfulness filled my heart; but I was bitterly disappointed. I hung up the phone and went to get dinner, needing to busy myself with something. Why would God have held out to us this dream home, only to withdraw it? Would he tease us?

This huge disappointment was going to be the beginning of our learning to adjust and readjust our dreams, to force our clenched hands open so God could fill them, to lean into his love, and to wait. Yes, we were to learn patience.

And so began our search for whatever home God would give us. Sometimes it takes awhile to let go of a dream and start all over again, especially when that dream held such a prominent place in our hearts. It would take time to look with enthusiasm once again for the home that God must be preparing for us.

Fortunately, other events were occupying our lives, events that would help to form a new direction.

3.
You Prepare a Table Before Me

SWEET AND SAVORY AROMAS of cinnamon and sage fill the house. A stuffed turkey has been slowly baking in the large white roaster, and in the oven are three pies: the traditional pumpkin, minced meat, and apple. Fresh baked rolls rest in two wicker baskets lined with blue napkins. The hands of the clock hanging beside the old cupboard are moving quickly toward noon.

Taking off my apron, I step into the dining room for one last check. The table is set for a family Thanksgiving meal, decorated with tableware holding precious memories: blue dinner plates collected from Ralph's grocery store in California when the children were young; tall, blue drinking glasses that were gifts from my daughter Sara; antique oil lamps from my father-in-law's collection—a silent reminder of his past presence at this table. Carefully penned name cards are attached to fall leaves from the yard, identifying the anticipated guests around the table. In front of the setting at Judd's seat lies an open Bible waiting for him to read before the meal begins. My heart is full as I anticipate the conversation, food, love, fellowship, and refreshment that will be shared around this table.

I believe the sense of anticipation that marked those early years here in Kansas helped us to recognize God's hand in the unfolding events. Looking back now, we clearly see that while we were in the process of walking by faith, God was setting our "table," and he was directing the hearts of people who would eat at this table with us. God, as the host, always sets the table for the ones who will be feasting together. He has the plans for that grouping, for the discussion at the table, and for the spiritual food he will serve.

THE GUESTS

From the very beginning, God brought the guests. Each guest had his and her own name card, as it were. Sometimes they were invited for the "toast," sometimes they came for the soup and salad, some came for the entrée, and some for the dessert. A few stayed for the whole meal and became the established community here on Kitten Creek Road.

The Reker family, who welcomed us to Kansas, had a big part in our first year of settling. They were here for the "toast." They understood our desires for ministry. George had worked with Judd before, and we knew of George and Sharon's love for family ministry. The Rekers were an integral part of all that we did in the early years.

The Bascom family pretty much stayed for the whole meal. They had returned from Ethiopia by way of Sudan only a year before we arrived in Manhattan. A revolution in their beloved Ethiopia had caused them to lose their ministry there. Here in the United States, their vision, like ours, had also been stirred by the L'Abri story and the writings of Francis Schaeffer. (Philosopher, theologian, missionary, and writer, Francis's books would be the center of many discussions, especially among college students in the 1970s and 80s.) The Bascoms had, meanwhile, settled in the nearby town of Riley.

And then there were the college students who each had a story, each had gifts, and each had been drawn to our "table." These students were also present for that important "first toast." Johnathan, the Bascoms' oldest son, in graduate school at K-State, was active in InterVarsity on campus. Gregarious and compelling, John began to gather other students to meet every other Saturday with his parents and the Rekers and us in our basement. At times, we were joined by the area director of Inter-Varsity, Steve Garber, who would bring young, thoughtful students from other colleges, as well.

Those early guests brought the joy and excitement of a great "toast" at the beginning of a meal. Anticipation! It was not long before this group was envisioning a L'Abri conference in the largest auditorium on the Kansas State campus. College students with fervor and youthful energy, coupled with adults who had life experience and vision, combined inspiration with our necessary dependency on God.

We had been in the rental home less than a year by the time this little group of students, the Rekers, the Bascoms, the Swiharts, and several other professors had planned and facilitated a conference at K-State's McCain auditorium. Creativity abounded. Some students with artistic ability created a brochure, others rounded up housing for conferees who could not afford a hotel room, and scholarships were offered. John headed the charge in communicating with the sponsoring organization. Seven-hundred and fifty people attended this conference.

That first year in the rental home much of the table was being set, and we began to jell as a committed group.

THE TABLE

What was God doing? What plans did he have for us here in this

Kansas town? As the Swiharts began to settle into life-in-transition, God was not only inviting the guests, but unbeknownst to us at the time, he was also preparing the table: a little farm on Kitten Creek Road.

Loss and waning health made it necessary for an elderly farmer, Oscar Fritz, to close down his decades of farming. Oscar had moved his family—his wife, Minnie, and their little son, Howard—to the farm in the early 1900s. Howard had continued to help with the farming long after marrying and moving close by to a home of his own. Minnie had died about eight years before we arrived in Kansas. Oscar, in his eighties by then, was very dependent on the help of his son.

When his son died unexpectedly of appendicitis, Oscar recognized the fact that he could no longer manage the farm. Putting his estate on the market, he moved to live with his daughter-in-law. I can only imagine the depth of Oscar's grief at giving up the farm where he had worked for the greater part of his life, leaving behind all he had built on this plot of land in the Flint Hills. Oscar had raised chickens, hogs, and dairy cows, and had grazed cattle and farmed milo. Minnie had planted lilacs, petunias, sweet William, and tulips. The basement and cellar still boasted jars of canned goods stored years earlier from her labors of love. Years of work, love, heartache, and joy had been lived out on that old farmstead.

At the same time that Oscar was winding down his life at the farm, we were beginning our venture of searching for the "right" place for a family-based ministry. The poor realtor who was helping us find this dream could only go by our vague specifications. I don't think we could actually spell out to her what we planned to do with this property, because we, ourselves, did not exactly know. How could we tell her we were shopping for a "vision"?

Our basic instructions were that it should be a large house on a few acres. In such a home, lots of people could come and go, and we could serve God somewhat as the Schaeffers had. However, as our realtor took us from one prospective property to another, we found the houses on a few acres were inadequate, and the large houses in town on small lots wouldn't work. Nothing was right.

One cold February morning, Sandy, our new realtor, called. We had been out looking several times already that week, and I could feel her exasperation.

"I am puzzled." Her sigh was almost a groan. "I am trying to find something for you, but I'm just not sure I understand exactly what you are looking for."

She had a right to be frustrated. Trying to find the kind of home we had said we were looking for, she had showed us homes in excellent condition. Any other client would probably have found at least one of the homes perfect. None had met our approval. We were rather reluctant to explain to this well-meaning lady that our vision was quite cloudy, and a big part of that vision depended not upon our rational requirements, but something more intuitive and God-directed. In fact, we did not know what we were looking for but believed we would "know" when we saw it.

One morning the children had left for school, and I was putting away the clean breakfast dishes, when the phone rang.

"Nancy, I may have something for you. This is a long shot, but someone in my office has listed property that you might be interested in." The house she described had two bedrooms, 950 square feet, but it was on one-hundred and sixty acres. Though it was a smaller house than we needed, and a larger property than we had ever considered, the price was close to what we wanted to spend.

I hung up the phone and called Judd. "OK, Judd. Are you sitting down? I have a little adventure for you. Can you meet Sandy and me at the realtor's office in a half hour?"

Silence on the other end of the line. How many times had we gone through this before? Did he want to take the time out of his day to look one more time? I knew he was hesitant to interrupt his day. There was a half foot of snow on the ground, too; not a particularly good day to be out of the office.

"What are we going to look at?" Judd asked.

"Well," I stammered. "It's not a large house; it is nine-hundred and fifty square feet. It's not on a small acreage, but on one-hundred and sixty acres. And..." Again I hesitated. "It has no indoor toilet."

Silence, again, on the other end of the phone. But one thing that Judd and I have in common is that we like adventure. He, also, was intrigued. Going to look at this place sounded like an adventure in itself.

A short time later, under a brilliant-blue sky, we stepped out of our realtor's Cadillac onto a snow-covered driveway and looked around. *Oh, my!* Nothing we had seen before even began to touch the magnificence of this place.

Sandy the realtor saw a dilapidated old farm: the huge unpainted barn, the leaning garage, the small white bungalow on the hillside, and the yards dotted with run-down sheds.

The scene we saw was a snow-covered Grandma Moses painting, and both of our spirits said, *Home!*

Yes! Our hearts were drawn. Our eyes saw a promise. This quaint old farm was where God wanted us.

Wanting to show us the acreage before we became disillusioned, Sandy took us wading through the snow to a wooded area beyond the house, up into the pastures, and back down to the little bungalow. We knocked the snow off our boots, then entered the back porch through the rusted screen door. Torn plastic covered the windows of the summer porch, and an old iron bedstead rested against the wall. Behind the kitchen door stood a crate turned on its end with a broken mirror above.

The old, white-porcelain sink and the cupboards had seen better days but were still in useable condition. A woodstove in the corner of the kitchen, with small square isinglass windows in its door, evidently had provided the heat during winter. A lone picture of Jesus knocking at the door hung in the otherwise-empty living room.

As we continued through the house, I saw possibilities. Even with no indoor toilet, large holes worn in the linoleum, and cobwebs and dust decorating the four-roomed house, this place tugged at our hearts.

Why did it stir within us a sense of coming home? Maybe we recognized the little name card God had placed that said "Swihart." Only God could have prepared our hearts for what was waiting on this table on Kitten Creek Road in Kansas.

As the snow began coming down in earnest, we made our way back to the car and headed to the realty office. "Yes!" we declared as we began the paperwork. "Yes, we will buy this house and property for the asking price, and we will buy it 'as is.'"

How do we see the hand of the Lord and know it is truly his hand? Perhaps this happens when we finally let go of our own dreams and hold out our empty, expectant hand to him. Perhaps it is the result of a lifetime of seeking to know him through his Word and listening to his Spirit, years of learning, of falling, of getting back up, but always of trusting.

I like to think that Psalm 23 is a promise for all of God's children: "A table Thou hast prepared before me." He does set a table for each of us, a particular place in this world, and the gift of guests who surround us. God's story written in each of our lives will be unique, but joining him at his table, anticipating the fellowship, and enjoying the food he has prepared will fill our stories with adventure.

4.
Looking Back

DOES GOD SET A TABLE before each of us and allow us to decline to come to the table? He is a gracious host. His love goes beyond our negative responses. He will not force us to come to the table, nor will he force us to sup with him.

Before I go forward with the story in Kansas, I must reflect on my California regrets. Regrets are not wholesome or healthy unless they produce something. We can learn from regrets and change our trajectory, our habits that may be at the root.

In Kansas, I was excited every day expecting to see God at work. I looked for it, I learned to see it. Knowing now how ever-present God is in my life in Kansas, what did I miss when I lived in California? Was God not there; or did I miss something?

I am sure that I missed it. But I am not sure what it was, because I wasn't looking for it. Oh, yes, I caught some of it, but I diminished it by grumbling, complaining, and wishing for something other.

Although I know I miss much of God's presence every day of my life, this chapter is a reflection on how much more often I failed to see him before we moved to the farm. Acknowledging my regrets can lead me to grow more attentive.

We lived in California "temporarily" for eleven years, and I was always looking for the escape clause.

I was seven months pregnant with my second child when I had my first introduction to the San Fernando Valley. Judd's sister Anita had picked thirteen-month-old Derrick and me up at the Los Angeles airport to take us to the home where we would live until we found a house to rent. Judd was making the trek by car from North Carolina, bringing our meager life possessions with him. With Derrick on my lap (no seat belts or child restrainers in those days) we descended the hill between Los Angeles and the Valley.

Anita was cheerfully chatting, but I had stopped listening. I was in a state of panic. "Oh, my dear Lord, so many people; so much concrete, so many buildings, and ... the smog. I am going to be lost in this place." I had grown up in Pennsylvania. I loved the green, the open fields, and the farms. Open spaces spoke to me of a loving and caring God. Here I was descending into a man-made material world, speeding traffic, blaring horns, millions of people, and an arid land that was green only if irrigated by the human inhabitants. I felt I was losing my soul.

I allowed my reaction to deprive me of the gift of seeing with God's eyes. He was inviting me to walk this new walk with him, and I didn't accept the gift of anticipating what this adventure with God would bring.

Maybe part of my uneasiness came from the hormonal imbalance of a very pregnant woman, or the fact that I had just traveled across the country with a toddler without the aid of my husband. But I was definitely not experiencing the thrill of an adventure with God, and I was not anticipating his presence in this new life. I was scared, homesick, and overwhelmed. The days that followed seemed to fulfill my initial reaction. In many ways I became wooden, bracing myself for what I was going to have to do and who I was to become in this new, strange world.

I missed the chance to flourish.

As I look back on those eleven years, I see that all my struggles did keep leading me, inch by inch, into a more mature relationship with my Father. But flourish? To flourish, you need to be working *with* God. I was being dragged, almost unaware that he was involved in what was happening.

That first year we struggled to get our feet under us. Judd worked three part-time jobs until he was hired full-time with the megachurch where we served. Three part-time jobs meant he was gone ... a lot.

I missed the gift of peace that passes all understanding.

We had been settled in our new home about three months when a fire surrounded the San Fernando Valley. Panic! I had a toddler at home, Judd was at work, my laundry was hanging on the line being dusted with black ashes floating down from the sky, and I had no car. The fire trucks flew past the house. Although Judd helped to fight the fires that surrounded his brother's home, our home was far from the danger of burning. But I was not becoming any more enthralled with my adopted environment.

I missed the gift of security that God was offering.

I lived more in fear of a life out of control than the quiet confidence that God was covering me with his presence.

As if the fires were not enough, we were to become more closely acquainted with another of California's environmental offerings. Our new baby, Dan, was three months old, and Derrick was a year and a half when we experienced the 6.8 earthquake centered in the San Fernando Valley. Judd and I were sound asleep in our front bedroom when the house began to shake violently. My first thought was of my babies down the hall, and I jumped up to go to them. But I could not walk. The floor was rolling like solid waves. I fell back into bed and prayed.

We had been warned about earthquakes. California was going to drop off into the ocean. It had been predicted, and some people were sure it would be soon. When the shaking stopped, I went directly to the nursery. Both babies were sleeping soundly. No trauma for them.

Our house had a little damage—dishes fallen out of the cupboards, bookcases knocked down—but nothing that could not be fixed. My psyche was another story. Concrete walls had fallen onto sidewalks. Bridges had collapsed. People had died. I, as the mother of two helpless babies, had been given a new mantle: I must, at all times, be aware of where my babies were, ready to grab them and take them to safety when the earth, which had always been my terra firma, should begin to threaten our lives again. A low-level anxiety filled my heart. I felt God had abandoned me.

I missed finding true refuge in the Solid Rock.

Our rough introduction to Southern California slowly faded into a routine, less dramatic lifestyle. We attended the megachurch where Judd worked, and we learned how to relate to others on Sunday, and how to develop some relationships. The redeeming aspects of those years for both of us were the friendships we forged through Judd's counseling center and a women's group that I led. We shared community in those groups that provided "home" for our souls.

Through the years in the Valley, two of our children were born, we were surrounded by our extended families, shared holidays, and created many, many wonderful memories. But my heart never felt at home. I was discontent with the "foreign" feel of my surroundings. I disliked the emphasis that I saw on materialism that seemed to pervade everything, even the church. I longed for a yard that would survive without constant watering (such a little thing). I wanted to go somewhere and not have to stand in a line or fight all the traffic every time I left the house. I felt like a prisoner during the smog alerts when the children were advised to stay indoors for the day, or when we could no longer allow our children to go alone to the park two blocks away because of the murders there.

Some people thrived on the Southern California lifestyle— good people I admired and loved. I, on the other hand, pled with God to remove us from this strange, foreign land.

The last three years of our California experience we stepped away from the megachurch and joined an unusual church family that met at a restaurant and welcomed those who would not darken the doors of a church. It was a mission church. We flourished in our new environment. This group with its understanding of church, its practice of community, its desire to grow as disciples of Jesus, gave us a model that we would pursue when we moved to Kansas. This experience inspired us to seek something similar, something that would grow deep into authentic spiritual community when we moved away from our California home.

As I reflect on those years I have a sense of remorse. I missed so much because of my discontentment.

In Acceptance Lieth Peace

In acceptance lieth peace,
  O my heart be still;
Let thy restless worries cease
  And accept His will.

Though this test be not thy choice,
It is His—therefore rejoice.

In His plan there cannot be
Aught to make thee sad:
If this is His choice for thee,
Take it and be glad.
Make from it some lovely thing
To the glory of thy King.
Cease from sighs and murmuring,
Sing His loving grace,
This thing means thy furthering
To a wealthy place.
From thy fears He'll give release,
In acceptance lieth peace.

–Hannah Hurnard

5.
Making a House a Home

WE BOLTED OUR DINNER, a sense of urgency and excitement in the air. The children had loaded the station wagon with buckets, hammers, scrapers and other odd implements needed for the evening's work. Judd, home from his now somewhat routine teaching duties at the university, had changed into his old jeans and wool shirt. As a last minute thought, I packed a blanket and pillow into the back. Late nights at the "new" old house made it hard for six-year-old Sara to get up early for school.

As we wound our way through the town and headed out into the country, we made plans. This particular night, the boys and Judd would be pulling up the linoleum in the living room. Sara and I would start in the kitchen, getting the walls ready for the blue patterned wallpaper I had chosen. At last I would have a blue kitchen.

The few homes along the gravel road to the farm sported well-kept yards and a certain orderliness. We were curious about our soon-to-be neighbors, and—as we found out later—they were curious about us. The word had already spread that we were from California, and they suspected we knew nothing about farming. The neighbors, who were invested in "keeping up" the neighborhood, watched the farm falling into disrepair over the years. How would these California transplants ever survive, let alone do a respectable job of keeping up a farm?

They had known the previous owners, the ones who had moved in with their belongings loaded on a wagon drawn by a team of horses. To the neighbors, half of them relatives, it was "Uncle" Oscar and "Aunt" Minnie, and their memories were still vivid in that old neighborhood.

Now was the time for new blood to reclaim this place, time to breathe life back into the home that had once been teeming with life and vitality, We had spent weekends scrubbing and cleaning out the cobwebs, loading out the forgotten contents of the basement, and taking pick-up loads to the Riley dump. With help from our newly acquired "extended God family," those very special young people who would come alongside to dream and create ministry here, we sent over twenty truckloads to that dump. The cost of buying the farm had been based on the acreage—160 acres—with no price attached to the house. Because of this, little had been done to the house to make it attractive to buyers. Had it been bought by a neighboring farmer, which everyone thought would happen, the house would have been more of a problem than an advantage.

However, the very fact the house had been ignored was a blessing to us. As we sifted through the belongings left behind in closets, corners, cupboards, basement, we also found the history of the home: the farm records that Oscar had meticulously kept, logging the sale of milk, eggs, etc., and the cost of feed and equipment. We found the booklet that the electric company had sent out to farmers, encouraging them to upgrade their homes with electricity; bags of flower bulbs that Minnie had stored in the basement; an old Crosley freezer with the directions for freezing produce and meat. We found an old wooden incubator, wire egg baskets, and the top of an antique kitchen cupboard. We were touched when we found a small room walled off from the rest of the cellar with rows of canned vegetables and fruit, probably Minnie's handiwork from years ago. The picture of Jesus hanging on the living room wall carried a message that this house had been blessed long before we were to live within its walls. Oh, we felt blessed also—sometimes overwhelmed, but blessed.

Spring began to unfold during our settling-in days, and Minnie's flower gardens, unkempt for years, began to produce pleasant surprises. *The Secret Garden* was one of my favorite books growing up; now I had my own "bit of earth."

As we drove up to the house that evening, we unloaded the car and entered the cold, empty house. Ah, it already felt like home. We had figured out how we would make a two bedroom house accommodate the five of us. Judd and I would take the larger bedroom which was entered through the bathroom. There was no toilet in the bathroom, just a sink and bath tub, but the outhouse had been adequate for the Fritz family, so we would make it work for awhile. From our bedroom, we could go to the boy's bedroom, from the boy's bedroom was a door to the living room where Sara would sleep on the couch until we could make a bedroom in the cellar for the boys. From the living room, we could go to the kitchen, and from the kitchen back to the bathroom, quite a simple floor plan. The early builders wasted no space on hallways or closets. Each bedroom sported a tiny closet with hooks to hang clothes. But we would make this work. Somehow, we loved this musty old house with its history, personality, and character.

We had brought a bucket of water from home (did I mention that there was no running water at the farm since the pipes

47

coming from the well a quarter mile away had rusted shut?). Once the walls were ready, Judd decided to help get the first couple of wallpaper sheets on the wall before we left that evening. We set up everything we needed to measure and cut and hang. After pouring the water into the old claw-foot bathtub, we measured our first sheet, rolled it, and put it in the tub to soak. While it soaked, we cut and rolled our next nine-foot sheet. Going back to the tub to get the first roll, we discovered that the tub was empty, and the water was spread out over the bathroom floor. Evidently, the old drain joints were coming apart and needed work before the tub would hold water.

"Rats! The evening has been a wasted," I muttered aloud, as I sopped up the water and threw the towel in the empty bucket. (Good intentions? Ministry?) "This shouldn't have to be so hard if we are working with you, Lord. It seems like we are doing all the work here," I grumbled.

This experience was only one of many lessons we would face in the days to come. Working with God doesn't mean that God does all the dirty work and we just watch what he does. It was hard work. Ahead of us lay many more lessons about living in a fallen world full of decay and weeds and an enemy who would love to discourage God's children as they try to reclaim parts of that fallen world for God's kingdom.

By 8:30 we were ready to head back down the gravel road, to a house that had running water where we could take our showers and get a night's rest. Tomorrow would hold more opportunities for resettling our "new/old house," more opportunities of working with God.

Years ago, I read Paul Tournier's book, *The Adventure of Living*. We were living the adventure of faith.

6.
A Well Story

AS THE SCHOOL BUS PULLED OUT of the drive, I began clearing the table of its breakfast remains. Without the luxury of a dishwasher, I filled the sink with hot soapy water and carefully slid the dirty dishes into the water. This dishwashing process had become therapy. And after six weeks of carrying water from town, I celebrated that we had running water from the faucet.

Shortly after we moved, we had located a spot near the house where Oscar, the original owner, had placed an old hydrant. When the well diggers finally came, it had not taken long before we had a functioning well. The aquifer was only sixty feet down into the earth, right near the back porch. A blessing, so it seemed.

The process of carefully running the dishcloth over each bowl, cup, and piece of silverware, then rinsing, drying and returning them to their rightful place gave me a sense of accomplishment. This became my contemplative time. But that morning I was troubled, my heart and mind in a battle.

The weekend had been frenetic, to say the least. Looking out the window I saw mud, weeds, work and more work. Entropy had set into this old farm, and although we had been working as hard as we could for the past five months, we were overwhelmed with all that still remained to be done.

My heart was heavy. We wanted to have a ministry. Instead, work was the focus of our lives. It took a lot to tame these tangled fields, overgrown yards, broken down fences, and dilapidated buildings. On weekends we had help from college students who seemed actually to thrive on the challenge. But during the week, our little family was faced with the stark reality of what we had jumped into with such enthusiasm. And all we had was our muscle. No machinery. After we had signed the papers for the farm, Oscar had sold all the farm equipment separately at an auction. All the equipment Oscar had used on the farm—tractor, plough, spreader, etc.—was gone. What we had in our possession were shovels, picks, rakes, the always-in-use brush clippers, and a newly-purchased old pickup truck to haul things.

The kitchen clean, the dishes put away, I slumped into the soft easy chair in the living room for "quiet time" with the best listener I have. And I had lots to say that morning. "Lord, I am confused. Our lives have become consumed with the farm, the buildings, the mud, and hard work! Did we not hear you right? Are we stuck here because of our folly, thinking that you were going to bless us with a ministry of serving others? Please, please let us know that we are where we should be, that you are in this with us." The lament and the pleading continued for awhile. I was trying to listen, but my thoughts were too loud to hear anything from him at the time. "I need to hear from you," I concluded. "I am willing to do what you want me to do, but I need to hear from you."

There are times when God responds in ways that shake us to our core. Times when we know, without a shadow of a doubt that he is speaking directly to his child. This was such a time, although the interpretation was not immediately apparent.

Feeling thirsty, I rose from my seat of lamentations and headed to the kitchen. Grabbing a glass from the cupboard, I turned on the faucet and held my glass out expectantly. But no water came from the tap—that tap which had been running freely while I had done my dishes, that tap for which I rejoiced earlier that morning. I froze. If God was speaking, he had my attention. But what was the message? Was God saying, "Get out of here. This farm was a big mistake"?

I dialed Judd's number at the University, collecting my thoughts. Yes, I had tried the other taps. There was *no* water coming from any of them. Obviously, at least to me, this was God's response to my plea for direction; it was no coincidence. But now I was faced with explaining all of this to Judd, who ultimately would feel the responsibility of determining the next step. Yes, we would discuss it and seek God's direction, but a man will often feel the burden of the final decision. We were now in this together.

"Judd, we have a problem." Tension, maybe a little panic, together with a sense of foreboding was probably conveyed in the tone of my voice. Judd always seemed to be able to balance my emotional extremes with an exaggerated calmness.

Silence. And then, "Okay, can you explain it to me?" After a short conversation, we decided to wait to call the well diggers or anyone else until we had time to assess the situation.

That evening we had a lengthy discussion as a family. With the last well, we had spent over a thousand dollars on one drilling that had seemingly been successful. Should we try again? Or should we assume God's message was that we should change directions, reevaluate this farm venture, and maybe pull the plug on it? But where would we go?

How could we start all over again? We delayed a decision for another day. Meanwhile, we were without water again, and that meant some adaptations we had learned so well those first six weeks. Find big containers, minimize bathing rituals, save water by using the outhouse. Back to the camping mode.

We started the next morning with a prayerful and very tentative approach. Now both Judd and I were listening to what God might be saying. No longer was I so loquacious with God. I would keep quiet and let him speak to me.

After I had cleaned the dishes and the kitchen as best I could, I grabbed my Bible and returned to my worn, comfortable chair. I allowed the Bible to fall open to where I had been reading in Isaiah, then settled my heart. My eyes fell upon words that seemed to come from the mouth of God directly to me.

Once again I was awestruck. Indeed, I understand the argument that we should never read verses from the Bible out of context. But I also know that the Word of God is "alive and powerful." And after walking with God as long as I have, I know that he will interact with us in ways that we understand, especially when we need direction, guidance, reassurance. The verses that jumped off the page that morning came to me almost audibly. I imagined Jesus sitting in the rocking chair beside me, his kind eyes gazing into my troubled heart. I have written the date, October 4, 1982 in the margin of my Bible.

> The afflicted and needy are seeking water,
> but there is none,
> And their tongue is parched with thirst;
> I, the Lord will answer them Myself,
> As the God of Israel I will not forsake them.
> I will open rivers on the bare heights,

And springs in the midst of the valleys;
I will make the wilderness a pool of water,
And the dry land fountains of water...

That they may see and recognize,
And consider and gain insight as well,
That the hand of the Lord has done this,
And the Holy One of Israel has created it.

–Isaiah 41:17,18,20

This was exactly the assurance I needed. God *was* in this. It *was* his land; we would be his stewards. He would provide not only the water that we were needing, but his Spirit, the Aqua Vitae, would bring the fruit and be the sustainer. Why? So that the glory would go to him.

Now we could go forward with assurance. So, how was he going to solve this, exactly?

Then began another learning curve.

As much as I hate to admit my naiveté, I dared to wish that we would find not only the needed water, but perhaps—could I even dare to believe—we would find oil?

Excitement had filled my whole being while my soul waited on tiptoe to see how God would fulfill this promise. He was going to "pour out" blessings. What did this mean? (The reality was that he was going to bless the land with an anointing of his Spirit.)

God also knew that we had little financial resources. He had always seemed to supply the Schaeffers, our inspirational models, with the money that would help them continue their ministry; would he not supply ours as well? What was God writing into the Swihart story?

We are often mystified by the twists and turns that experience takes. How often I have learned that I must let go of my expectations and desires, and trust what he is doing. In reading David Benner's 2002 book, *Sacred Companionship*, I am reminded that God is interested in all the aspects of our earthly lives, but his perspective is eternal, and his interest is in our personal transformation into who we were uniquely created to be as his children.

He was leading us very gently on this journey.

Judd had called the drilling company as soon as we made the final decision to move ahead. After talking to neighbors to find out where their wells were located, we had chosen several spots where we thought there might be an underground stream. First, though, we wanted to make sure that the old well was indeed dry.

When the drillers showed up early the next day with the impressive drilling rig, I was ready. Judd and I had decided to have them dig once again, but deeper this time, at the current well hole. The two workmen set up the rig, and the drill began to churn its way down through the hole and past the bottom. I didn't want to miss what I knew God would do. A miracle, right in front of my eyes. As I watched, I leaned forward expectantly, my eyes fastened on that noisy contraption, expecting any minute that there would be a great discovery. If you know anything about well drilling, you are aware that the drill today spins its way effortlessly through rocks, clay, and dirt. This old one, however, ground, sputtered, clanked, and smoked as it methodically chiseled its way downward.

After an hour of watching from a standing position, I went back into the house and retrieved my dad's old fishing stool that I had civilized with paint and stenciling. I placed it as close to the men and their machine as I could, so I had a good view, but far enough away that I would not interrupt their hard work. With the two workers and I, the large drill, and the truck all sandwiched between the lilac bushes and the bank of a hill, I was probably more a part of the operation than these professionals wanted. The October sun was gently shining on my back, and besides the upheaval of dirt and the noise of the machine, I was oblivious to any other distractions or the driller's discomfort. This was my post. So sure that there would be a miraculous discovery of water, I was glued here, wanting to be in on the great celebration.

Finally, after what seemed like hours, the drill was silenced, and the men came over to discuss what they had found. Our old well had simply been a small aquifer that we had drained in the last few months, and it would take possibly years to fill again.

So, where to drill next? With our direction, they moved the drill down by the garage and set up again. I could not afford to sit all day and watch the machine that was going to, somehow, hit the water supply that God had promised. I had household chores waiting, so I reluctantly carried my stool back into the house. From the kitchen I could hear the clanking of the drill as it went after that elusive water.

"No water in that spot!" came the report. Once more they moved the rig, this time across the gravel road. The day waned. After eight hours of drilling, it grew quiet down in the field. The men had quit for the day ... without the promised water supply. I was disappointment, but not discouragement. God had promised.

Yes, our faith was being tested, yet I could not doubt Cod's commitment to us.

All this drilling was costing us money for which we had not planned. It was as though time had suspended, and we were waiting for it to begin again. "Wait" is a word and a stance that has become familiar to us over the years.

The next morning, the drillers came to the back door and knocked. Head down, moving from one foot to the other, the boss finally looked at me and said, "Supposing we choose the sight to drill this morning? We would like to move farther down in the field. It may be farther from the house, but we think that area is more promising."

At a loss for any other suggestion, I gave them my permission and blessing. "You are the experts. Go for it!"

Again came the chug of the motor as they started the drill and the clanking of metal as it hit rocks. I continued my clean-up in the kitchen. *God will do what he is going to do without my observation*, I reasoned.

In an hour or two the drilling came to a halt and two drillers appeared at the back door.

"Water! Lots of water!" was the triumphant report. They acted as though they had hit a gold mine. Having dug hundreds of wells, they appeared almost disbelieving. Most wells in our area were producing one-half to four gallons a minute. This well was producing more than a hundred gallons per minute! They were not sure exactly how much, because they could only measure up to one hundred gallons per minute. It became known as one of the best wells, if not the best, in the area.

"Abundantly more than we ask or think" says Ephesians 4:20. We were committed now. How was God going to create and sustain this ministry? How would we work with him in the coming years? Who would he bring along to join us? The future was entirely in his hands. Forward we would go.

7.
A Name

UNTIL NOW, THIS WELL STORY had been a private, family matter. First, it meant that we would not have to haul water; second, it meant that we had God's affirmation on our calling at the farm; third, and most affirming to me, was the promise of God's blessing. I saw this land as belonging to God, and we as his stewards.

Finding water was only the beginning. We had to hire someone to dig the line from the well to the house, a distance of about three-hundred yards. But who was complaining at this point? God had proven himself faithful in giving us this unusual well, and we were beginning to understand the depth of his love and the steadfastness of his character. At this point in our lives we thought we had withstood all the tests and had grown into maturity through these tests; but in many ways we were still babes learning how to live in a trusting relationship with our Father.

And soon, the well story began to take on more significance.

Saturday evening our living room crowded with eager, creative, college students along with several college professors and a retired missionary couple. After meeting for over a year and a half, we had somewhat jokingly called ourselves "The Group at the Place with a Plan." But, it was time to define ourselves. As a group, we had already planned and orchestrated a L'Abri conference at Kansas State University, and we were now preparing to follow up by hosting a Spiritual Dynamics Conference at the farm. But our rag-tag group needed a name to identify us as we sent out brochures and contacted others. We now had a base of 700 names from the L'Abri Conference.

Of course, I was the big proponent of a name that had something to do with the well. "This was God's affirmation of what we are doing here on the farm already. And a promise of his Spirit poured out. Surely the name should have something to do with water."

Lots of water images were tossed around: Living Water (already taken), Water of Life, and finally, Wellspring began to emerge as the likely candidate. Most of those present came on board, but Judd was dragging his feet. Since he was an important part of this decision, we kept brainstorming. We wanted not just a consensus, nor a majority, but a unanimous decision.

In the middle of our discussion, the telephone rang and Judd jumped up to answer it. The call was coming from California. Our former pastor, Gordon Mollett, one of the godliest men we had ever known, was on the line. Judd had served on the steering committee of that little church which was, even now, our model for how to do church.

When Judd hung up the phone that evening, he came back into the living room chuckling. "Okay, you guys, I give up." Before he hung up Gordon had signed off with, "Remember, Judd, Jesus promised that from your innermost being will flow rivers of living water."

"I concede. 'Wellspring' it will be!" announced Judd.

And so began a new dimension to the place and to this group

who were gathering at this place. We had a name. It was a name that would be our identity, but it was also a name that continually reminded us of the source from whence would flow our power, our heart, and our vision. We were committed to listening to that source as we made our plans. He was to be the well from which we gained our sustenance.

8.
A Jitterbug/Slow-Waltz Romance

I SHOULD HAVE REALIZED IT when we were dating; but not until we had been married for awhile did I finally admit Judd and I were not moving to the same musical beat. Although neither of us went to dances in our youth, I can recognize the dance steps. If I were to visually describe our marriage, I would say it appears that Judd is doing a jitterbug while I am doing a slow waltz.

Judd wakes up thinking in lists. I wake up still dreaming. Judd pops into the shower; I stumble to the coffee pot. Judd wants breakfast immediately; I could wait until midmorning before I need any food. In many of our decisions, while Judd acts, I am still thinking.

An old friend from our California years, Dallas Willard, once described Judd as "a man with both feet on the ground." In my early years, I was described as being "too heavenly minded to be any earthly good." Today, Judd is leading a Sunday School class discussing practical day-to-day living from Proverbs. I am leading a ladies' study group discussing spiritual disciplines.

When we tried to co-author Judd's book, *How Do You Say I Love You,* Judd gave me the idea for writing one of the first chapters. After taking baby Sara to our neighbor to watch for several hours, I sat down and thought, and thought, and thought. By the time Judd got home that evening, I had written a paragraph. I was fired. Judd, on the other hand, said, "I am going to write now," and every time he sat down, he wrote and wrote and wrote. In a few months he had written a book.

You get the idea. We are each cut from different fabrics. So how did these fabrics join together to make something cohesive and usable? I would say that it took a good pair of scissors and lots of thread, both in the hands of the Tailor himself.

Judd's love for Proverbs comes from his appreciation of true wisdom, a gift that has paved the way for his counseling ministry. He seems often to innately understand issues and how to address them. My love for the spiritual disciplines has helped ground me as a follower of God. Although I tend to be naïve, I have clung to the promise in James: "If any of you lack wisdom, let him ask of God who gives to all men liberally." And God gave me Judd.

Our strengths can also be our weaknesses. We discover that truth every time we get a little overly invested in doing something "my own way."

"Two are better than one because they have a good return for their labor," says Ecclesiastes 4:9. This has proven true in our marriage. However, verse 12 contains the secret to a couple's success: Three are even better, for "a cord of three strands is not quickly torn apart."

We had a huge learning curve ahead of us when we tried to put our differences together to create a ministry out of our home. I was prepared to be the one at home, the one who would be the hostess, the one always present. Judd's vision, however, was to have me enter the work force and help with the finances as soon as the children were in school. Marriage and ministry were caught in the crosshairs.

So, what does ministry have to do with marriage? When I was teaching at the Christian college, I would often share with the students an article by Mark Lau Branson: "Marriage as Sanctification" (published in the March/April 1984 issue of *Radix Magazine*). Branson's premise is that the marriage covenant puts us in one of the most unique positions to work out our sanctification. He wrote:

> To move beyond a life set on power and control to a life of servanthood, contemplation, and vulnerability makes the work of the Spirit more readily available. There have been times when Christian marriage provided a profound witness for the Kingdom. Perhaps that can again happen—marriages providing a glimpse of the salvation offered by life in Christ: partners bearing witness to wounds that have been healed, priorities that have been rearranged, values that have been challenged, suffering that has been redeemed, lifelong relationships that furnish love and hope.

Dying to expectations and dreams is not easy. Yet, when our spirits and souls accept that we are truly loved by almighty God, when we can trust the partner that he has given us, and look back to that old mantra of "faith-rest," we will find that something new and maybe even better will be wrought.

Yes, Judd and I are two separate individuals, but instead of our differences being a deterrent or an obstacle in our marriage, they have enriched and broadened our individual sanctification and our outreach to others.

9.
A Personal Lesson In Obedience

GOD USED MY SUBMISSION to Judd's desire for me to work by not only expanding my life with the enrichment of new knowledge, new friends, and new horizons; he also delved into my personal handicaps.

I was raised by a mother who loved performance, and we greatly benefited from her encouragement and belief in us. She was an intelligent and progressive woman. She filled her daughters with the belief that we could achieve whatever we wanted. It was not a "pushy" kind of belief, but a supportive belief. I never felt handicapped by being a woman.

From the time her children could speak, she was training us to be before audiences. My first memory of performing for an audience still, after all of these years, plays like a short video clip repeating in my mind: I am stepping off the stage, down the big brown steps. As I pass the tall pews filled with adults I see them delightedly laughing and clapping. I march back to where my father sits and cuddle up to him, making room for my almost four-year-old brother to climb up beside me.

I could fill in the details only later as my parents recounted the story. Mom had prepared Sherwood, my big three-and-a-half year old brother, and me to sing "Jolly Old Saint Nicholas" at the Christmas Eve service in our little country church. The night of the service, however, Mom was in the hospital after delivering my new little sister. Now we all know that little girls (and boys) who are two-and-a-half can be quite unpredictable, and unpredictable I was that evening.

Poor Daddy, who had never really been part of the training, had sent us up front to do whatever it was that Mom had prepared us to do. We had practiced singing "Jolly old Saint Nicholas lean your ear this way, don't you tell a single soul what I'm going to say ... All the stockings you will find hanging in a row, mine will be the shortest one, you'll be sure to know." We did fine until we got to the last line when I heard my big brother sing to Santa, "Mine will be the shortest one, you'll be sure to know." I knew that my socks were smaller than Sherwood's. Why would he say that his were the shortest? I had been singing in our practices that *mine* would be the shortest one, never hearing what he had been singing until this crucial moment. So with no delay and through the rest of my brother's determined solo, I placed myself in front of his face and protested, "No, Shawy, *mine* will be the shortest one!"

Our audience, of course, loved it!

But little girls grow up. Through the years my brother and I sang at churches, schools, and talent shows. My sister joined us when at last she could carry a tune. Perhaps it was because we had moved so many times (I went to seventeen different schools in my years of schooling) that I grew into a very self-conscious teenager with terrible performance anxiety. After my brother went away to college, we formed a girl's trio with our cousin Sharon, winning a national contest, singing at Bible conferences, camps, and churches. Yet, I suffered physically and emotionally from terrible anxiety.

Finally, I made a vow. "God, if you will not heal me, I will not put myself in front of people again. Surely you can use me behind the scenes." And so for years I happily gave up my life of performance. I found fulfillment in teaching younger people and in supporting a husband who was comfortable in front of people. I was very happy on the sidelines, not facing the fact that underneath this complacency lay a sense and a history of failure ... failure to overcome a debilitating insecurity. Would God always let it lie dormant?

God has a way of throwing curves, just when you think you have arrived. The children were in school and we had a ministry that I could work at, right out of my own home. I had dreams and visions of how this would look. We would grow the ministry like the Schaeffers did L'Abri—albeit a Swihart/Wellspring kind of L'Abri.

Our money was tight, and it began to be very clear that Judd was hoping I would help with the income now that I no longer had preschoolers. Wanting to stay home, I tried desperately to find a happy middle.

Kathy, one of the young women who were part of the growing Wellspring ministry, dreamed and plotted with me. Since I had a small flock of sheep at the time, maybe we could have a wool and craft outlet. Outside of the fact that I was not, or ever have been a "crafty" person, I was still more than willing to try. Or, we could set up a small antique business out of one of the buildings here on the farm. Or, still believing that God could provide in miraculous ways, maybe one of my brother's financial schemes would bring in the windfall that he was expecting. He was more than willing to share with me if I invested just a small amount.

I had two deeply heart-felt issues against going to work: 1) I had made a commitment to God to focus on the ministry here at the farm. It was a vow I had made from which I could not walk away; and 2) with all that was going on here at the farm, with the boys in sports at school, and with Judd working on his Ph.D. while teaching full-time at the University, our family was stretched thin. I felt responsible for holding the family together; seeing that clothes were clean, folded, and where everyone could find them; having meals ready; in general, keep on track with everyone. I feared our family would fall apart if I was not there.

At times like these, married partners realize that even though we think we are on the same page, we may actually be reading different books. Judd saw the need for more income, and there was no reason in his mind for me to stay home with the children in school. Oh, how I pled with the Lord to change Judd's heart, to make him see what I was seeing.

My children were growing up; and even though I was very content being a stay-at-home mom, my husband, Judd, needed me to go to work full time. Since English was my undergraduate degree, I finally landed on a plan for my future. After much prayer and thought, I started back to school for a masters in American and British Literature. I was excited about getting back into reading, reading, and reading.

My first graduate class in literature, however, was to be life-changing for me, though not necessarily from the content of the class that semester. I had bought my textbooks the day before. That morning I saw my children off to school, got the house in order, and went to class with great enthusiasm. Ah ... I was a student again in a field that I loved. The professor went over all the requirements, handed out calendars, and laid out the plan for the semester. It was all great until he finally singled out the several grad students in the class. "Each of you will teach an hour-long class this semester. I will give you the topic, you will do the research, and then you will teach the rest of the class on what you have learned."

I left class in pure terror that day. My heart was pounding. Blood seemed to drain from my body. What was I to do? I had taught kindergarten, first grade, junior high, but those were little kids. These were peers. My first thought was, "Well, this was fun. Now I have to plan on some other way of entering the job market. And, by the way, God, I prayed about this. You led me here. What am I to do now?"

God seemed to say, "Try me. See what I will do. Don't quit."

I can honestly say this was one of the greatest growth periods in my entire life because I learned something through the next few months that was to change the way I lived out what I thought I truly believed.

The verses that surfaced for me in those first days of fear were verses that I said over and over to myself in the next few months. Their truth had to sink into my very being, into my subconscious, into the way I conducted my thought life, my daily habits. As I walked out to the barn to do my chores, I repeated them. Driving to school every day I would repeat them, tapping the steering wheel over and over. As I walked across campus, I reminded myself. Over and over and over. And those verses grew roots down into my innermost being.

"He is in me."

"Greater is he that is in me than he that is in the world."

"He has not given us the spirit of fear, but of power, and of love, and of a sound mind."

Things slowly began to change, not only in me, but also in the way I saw others. As I walked across campus every day, I began to see those young college students in a different light. If

God loved me and knew me so intimately that he was willing to live in me, how much he must love that girl there in the green jacket and that unshaved boy in front of me. He had known them and loved them in their mother's womb. He knew what they had had for breakfast that morning. He held out to them everything he had given to me. As I smiled at them or as I simply passed by, I could be a tangible presence of God ... maybe not perceptible to them in a concrete way, but nevertheless I carried his presence into their world.

I found that life was less and less about me. That had always been the issue with my performance anxiety. How was I doing? How well did I measure up to expectations? How perfect and above reproach could I be?

Semesters have a way of coming to a close, and my first semester of grad school was following the typical pattern. My day to lecture was approaching. Was I going to humiliate myself, or was I to find the "power and love and strong mind" that God had held out to me in his promise? The topic of my presentation in class was to be something on the Puritans. So, being family oriented, I chose the theology of family in Puritan life. With this topic, I could share with the class something of his love and plan.

As I walked to the front of the class that day, I breathed a silent prayer. Give me love, God, a love for these students that surpasses the focus on myself, a love that overcomes the fear I have for my own selfish needs. For the first time in decades, I stood in front of my peers and spoke from my head and my heart. I not only loved the message that I was delivering, but I loved my audience, not with *my* love but with the love of my Helper.

Driving home that day, I rejoiced. "Oh, God, it is all about You!" I remembered a song I used to sing in college with my friend Cheryl. We would find an empty practice room on campus and she would pound out the notes on the piano as we sang from the hymn book. Now, with my hands on the steering wheel and my heart in the clouds, I humbly yet jubilantly sang that song: "Without him, I would be nothing, without him I'd surely fail...."

Bottom line, I went to work. First I taught at Kansas State University, then ended up spending the rest of my career (yes, career that I had never sought, but which God used) at Manhattan Christian College, which has a dual-degree program with the university. My job created an extension to our farm ministry. I learned I could be a hostess in the classroom as well as at the farm.

Henri Nouwen's book, *Reaching Out* helped me to see how important hospitality is as a lifestyle—in the classroom, in the home, in daily life. He wrote:

> Hospitality therefore means primarily the creation of a free space where the stranger can enter and become a friend instead of an enemy ... not to change, but to give space ... where strangers can enter and discover themselves as created free (pgs. 54-55).

Yes, I could be a hostess, not only on the farm, not only in the classroom. I was learning how to expand my understanding of calling. How does marriage, ministry, work, and life in general look when God is sanctifying our lives, continually drawing us upward and inward?

10.
Praise the Lord, the Drought Is Over!

DURING THE FIRST YEAR, besides settling into the house, we focused on the old barn. It was big; and we could envision it empty. But that first year took patience and vision. The hay, which was stacked to the ceiling, had been auctioned off; however, the farmer who bought it was taking his time hauling it away. But we had a goal. We could use this barn for gathering people. Certainly, it could even house a weekend conference.

One of the first activities held in that old barn was a winter meeting of K-State InterVarsity. By that time, a small space in the center of the barn floor had been cleared of hay, and the students arranged bales for seating. They huddled in winter coats, mittens, scarves, singing along with a couple of guitars, their faces lit by battery-powered lanterns. An aura of camaraderie and adventure embraced the students. In this simple, unassuming environment, they were one.

When the hay bales had finally been claimed by those who had bought them at the auction, there was still much work to do before the barn could be used for a more-formal meeting. We hosted work days every Saturday. While Sara and I served drinks, snacks, and meals, many of the group who had joined us were out whacking weeds, tearing down dilapidated buildings, and loading out hay. Many exciting experiences and entertaining stories came from those infamous workdays.

Judd, Derrick, Dan, and several of the other guys had taken the challenge of cleaning out loose hay from the hayloft floor of the barn. Armed with pitchforks and large brooms, in the cool of the morning they donned dust masks then began to sweep, shovel, and move the hay towards the sliding door that opened to the barnyard below. The old white pick-up was positioned directly under the opened door. As soon as the truck bed was full, they hauled the hay away, dumped it, and came back for more. The operation progressed smoothly—that is until someone noticed a black snake slithering away. The snake slid under another pile of hay, so from then on, it was a game of "shovel and pick carefully with your eyes wide open."

I was not there to see it, but I'm told Judd became the center of attention as he suddenly danced across the hay, shaking his leg vigorously. He had disrupted the snake's hiding place when, in defense, the snake wrapped its long slithery body around Judd's left leg and rode the leg across the barn floor until Judd was able to dislodge him. To this day, Judd has disdain for snakes.

We discovered other articles besides snakes while we were cleaning the barn. Many of those items now decorate the barn walls: old reins, doubletrees, leather fly nets, snaffle bits, draft horse harnesses. The history of the farm lay under all that hay. We treasured these finds.

After the hay was cleared out, and the objects we wanted saved were rescued, the women took their turn. We never actually got rid of all the dust; but we tried. We wiped down the walls which were covered in cobwebs and hay seed. We swept and mopped as well as we could.

And then came the furnishing, such as it was. Our first chairs were old desk chairs. We bought a whole truckload that the University was disposing of, for a dollar apiece. The desks made ideal seats for a conference. It was easy to take notes, and conferees could store their purses and books on the shelf under the seat. We garnered a music stand that leaned a little, but would hold a speaker's notes. Our ingenious students of architecture were able to add lighting since the barn came with its own electrical box.

We were ready for our first conference in the barn!

That conference weekend is summed up by one poignant memory. We were in the final day of that first Spiritual Dynamics Conference. Donald Mostrom, an author from New England, had come to share with us. Don had recently published the book, *Intimacy with God*, and was also sharing from a book he was currently working on, *Spiritual Privileges You Didn't Know Were Yours*. We were walking with Don from the house to the barn for the final morning service. A sudden downpour engulfed us. It had been sprinkling, but now it was pouring. Discouragement dampened my spirit as I tramped through the mud with our guest speaker. However, Dr. Mostrom reacted to the drenching with exhilaration.

"Praise the Lord," he shouted as we walked up the hill to the barn that Sunday morning, "the drought is over!"

I looked at him in disbelief, but also relief.

Forty to sixty guests had come to spend the weekend. Some stayed in town, others at the farm in tents or on cots in the swept-out and hosed-down granary. Dr. Mostrom had the privilege of sleeping in the farmhouse in Sara's bedroom while she bedded on the floor of Judd's and my room.

After all our careful planning and preparation for this conference, it had rained the entire weekend. We had planned some exciting and fun times, such as a trail hike, Frisbee golf in the pasture, a volleyball game in the front yard. But instead, for most of the weekend we huddled in the barn.

Use of the barn came with limitations. The barn had no kitchen, so we supplied meals from the farmhouse kitchen. Young families with small children attended the conference, and we provided childcare for them in our living room. Our basement bathroom served as the main bathroom for the conference. In fact, the entire, tiny house became an extension of the conference.

By Saturday morning, in the kitchen we were almost wading in mud dragged in by constant traffic. By noon of the second day, the basement had flooded. From the bottom of the steps to the bathroom, we had set up an improvised "bridge" created from an old wooden ironing board that had been stored in the basement. (Creativity flourishes when there are few alternatives.) The living room nursery was cluttered and dirty, but dry.

We invited Don Mostrom to be our first guest speaker for several reasons. The first year together our group had studied—and been challenged by—*The Dynamics of Spiritual Life: An Evangelical Theology of Renewal* by Richard Lovelace. As we read Lovelace's acknowledgments, we discovered that an individual, Don Mostrom, had been one of Lovelace's primary mentors. Then, when the Bascom family traveled to New England to attend a Peniel Bible Conference, they came back renewed, refreshed, and desiring to hear more from the keynote speaker, Don Mostrom. We were thrilled when this man from the East Coast agreed to come to our poor, humble farm to join us for a weekend and share his thoughts from a book that he was working on at the time, *Spiritual Privileges You Didn't Know Were Yours*.

We were deluged that weekend, but not only with rain. We

had found joy in working together as a young community. We had studied together, planned together, and were now working out the individual gifts of each member. From cooking to nursery, from creating song sheets to leading the singing, from registration to clean-up, we each used our gifts.

Our children had been assigned their own important tasks: Derrick was to park cars, Dan and Derrick created the Frisbee golf course and blazed the trails for hiking; Sara at seven years old was appointed "the chief smiler" which she carried out with aplomb. Together, our community had been sitting at the feet of a spiritual giant as he challenged us and encouraged us with spiritual blessings from God's heart.

It is not always in the physical comfort of our surroundings that we find the presence of God. He was there as we waded to the bathroom, as we mopped the muddy kitchen floor or sat huddled in the barn instead of doing all the fun activities we had planned. Grace and joy abounded in the presence of the others who had gathered with us.

That weekend was an unwrapping of God's presence in community. Yes, in the midst of the mundane the sun was shining. Thus, the exclamation, "Praise the Lord, the drought is over!" was the capstone that crowned our weekend.

11.
Fire In Them Thar Hills

IT IS A TRUTH UNIVERSALLY ACKNOWLEDGED (at least in Kansas) that if there is a pasture, it must be burned. We were advised of this truth after we bought the farm: ranchers burn pasture as a non-chemical way to keep brush from taking over the prized tall-stem grass. And so began our fire stories: "Let us tell you about our first experience with burning when we had the K-State extension guys come out to help us."

Being novices, we were very nervous about this idea of walking through a pasture, spreading a line of fire behind us, and watching the flames leap hungrily at the tall, dry grass. So, for our first pasture burning, we turned to the Kansas State University extension agents for guidance. Two experts agreed to come out and help us take charge of managing pasture the Kansas way.

We were to start the burn at one o'clock, right after lunch, and we were a little on edge. Never before had we experienced something like this: intentionally burning forty acres of our own land. Judd, however, came home from work encouraged. Just before he left the office, he had been stopped by his friend and colleague, Ken.

"Judd," said Ken, "in my devotions this morning I read

Isaiah 43:2. 'When you walk through the fire, you will not be scorched, nor will the flame burn you.' I'm claiming this verse for you!"

We had recruited another friend, Mike, to help with the burn, and he arrived eager and ready. By the time our extension agents, Fred and Joe, arrived with the official truck sporting a large water tank and gas motor in the truck bed, we were ready. Judd had amassed what fire-fighting tools we had: shovels, rakes, a water sprayer backpack, and a few burlap bags. The men were ready to go, but Judd was still concerned. A steady breeze was building—one that had not been forecast—at times gusting to twenty to thirty miles an hour.

"We're not going to burn in this wind, are we?" Judd questioned Fred, the one who had assumed the lead. "This little wind is no problem," came Fred's confident assertion. "We'll be fine. I've never lost a fire in all the years I've been doing this."

So we headed across Kitten Creek and up to the pasture that was to be burned. Weary already, my legs felt like lead as I plodded up the steep, rough road through the cedars. We followed the truck working its way over rocks and around trees. Branches scratching the sides of the government truck sounded like fingernails scraping over a blackboard. The sound set my nerves on edge.

Finally we got up the hill to the pasture. The men agreed that, since the wind was blowing from the south, they would do a back burn around the north end of our pasture. This would prevent the fire from burning into the pasture to our north when we lit the rest of our pasture. "We'll build a perimeter," they decreed, "around the field to prevent the fire from going across to the neighbor's field." Judd and I could only trust their wisdom and experience. We certainly did not want to burn our neighbor's land.

"Nancy, you take that shovel and go across the fence on the neighbor's. The four of us will start the fire over here by the brush that is growing alongside the fence. Keep an eye on the grass on your side. If you see anything coming through, put it out with the back of your shovel." They gave me a quick lesson on how to use the back of the shovel to beat out the fire.

I grabbed the shovel, worked my way through a little brush, eased between the barbed wires and set up my post. A quick glance at the pasture where I was standing revealed a tall, thick, dry stand of grass that seemed to extend as far as I could see.

On the side of the fence opposite me, Fred had a rake to spread the fire; Judd and Mike were armed with water backpacks and shovels to put it out when it reached the desired width.

Joe took his torch and began to set fire to the grass along the brush. In what seemed like seconds, the wind gusted and fire began creeping under the fence. As soon as it touched the tall grass, it flared into a wild, unstoppable force.

Frantically, I pounded the fire with my shovel, but it was moving too rapidly for one person to control. "It's coming through! I need help!" I screamed. The barbed wire between us impeded the men, and by the time Judd could climb over the fence to help me, the fire was spreading well beyond us. The wind and dry grass were playing a game of "catch me if you can."

In a bit of a panic, the experts reasoned that this fire was going to take more than humanpower. Quickly cutting the five strands of barbed wire, they jumped into the truck, drove through the fence line, and raced to get ahead of the fire.

Joe, riding in the back of the pick-up had started the gas motor to the water sprayer and was ready to wet down the burned grass. However, with the grass so heavy beyond the fire, they could not see the terrain underneath it. After only a few hundred yards, they ran up on a layer of sharp rock and immediately punctured both left tires.

The truck was stranded, and the fire was heading straight for it. We could hear the gas motor for the water sprayer chugging away. The only course of action the two could take was bail out and run for safety. As the fire blazed over the truck, we braced for an explosion. But as the hungry flames continued their journey north, we gawked with amazement. The tuck sat there, miraculously intact.

The fire burned on, headed toward the neighbor's shed about a half-mile north. We must get help—now! I ran across our unburned pasture to warn the neighbors whose property bordered ours to the east and to ask them to call the fire department.

Judd ran down toward our house to get more water. The other three men stayed and did what they could with shovels and backpacks of water.

My once-leaden legs pumped full of adrenalin. I swear, I ran like a gazelle, at least the most like a gazelle I had ever—or will ever—run: over acres of ground, down into the hardwoods, under another fence and up the hill to the neighbor's.

Fortunately, the neighbor was home—quite unconcerned and unaware—sunning herself. I shouted to get her attention, warning that our fire had gotten away. She jumped up and disappeared to call the fire department. I headed back to the fire.

Judd, who had run down through the pasture and come out on Kitten Creek Road, had passed a neighbor driving her pick-up truck home. Seeing his apparent distress, she stopped and asked if she could help.

Struggling to catch his breath, Judd gasped, "We've lost a

fire and it's growing fast! Can you give me a lift home so I can get some water, and then can you take me back?" We had heard farmers tell stories of grass fires getting out of hand; surely this Kansas lady knew what to do.

Instantly she was on task, telling Judd to jump in the truck.

By the time they returned with water-filled buckets and trash cans, getting to the burning field by a circuitous route up another gravel road, they found the firemen had cut the fence so the fire crews could start putting out the fires.

The teenage children of the land's owner had driven their little red sports car out to survey the damage our fire had done. Chiding us and joking about a lawsuit, they seemed to find the whole incident amusing.

Firemen cannot leave the scene of the fire until it is completely out, so we waited for the final declaration. Finally, all was clear, and the group of us began to exit the pasture where the firemen had cut the fence. The fire truck led the way. I had jumped in our neighbor's truck, and she followed directly behind the fire truck. The little red sports car followed closely behind us. Heading out through the fence, the driver of the fire truck realized he could not make the sharp turn onto the gravel road, and without warning began to back up. Of course, our neighbor quickly put her truck into reverse and backed up also … into the little red sports car.

We had a new issue at this point. The teenagers were no longer in a jovial mood. The front of their sports car was quite smashed. That probaby was the first time the police had written up a traffic-accident report in the middle of a pasture. Trying to figure out what address to put on the report, and deciding whether or not to ticket us for not wearing our seatbelts, made this report even more extraordinary.

After it was all over, we sat at our kitchen table drinking lemonade with the "experts." We had successfully burned over sixty acres of our neighbor's pasture and none of our own.

Judd jokingly told Fred, who taught classes at the university, "Man, you are going to have some story to tell your students tomorrow!"

Looking thoughtfully at his half-empty glass of lemonade, Fred didn't crack a smile. He just groaned and said, "I am not going to tell a soul about this day!"

12.
The Fire We Did Not Set

DURING OUR THIRTY-FIVE YEARS on the farm, carrying out "good" burns for natural brush control, we've had enough "wild" experiences to fill another book. The wildest was the one fire we did not set, and it was potentially the most destructive.

Oblivious to the drama going on at home, Derrick and I were winding up a day as students at Kansas State University. Following the familiar road through the countryside to the little town of Keats, we felt revived from the stress and demands of the day. As in every fall, the leaves were changing again into yellows, reds, and gold, and the prairie grass to shades of purple, red, and orange. A steady wind was blowing from the south across the fields, and the grasses and leaves danced to its rhythm. The spectacular colors of fall filled us with a sense of peace.

Sometimes on these drives I would stop to pick a bundle of tall grasses along the roadside, to take home and place in a large vase on the kitchen table.

But today, as Derrick and I rounded the corner into Keats, we forgot everything else when we saw a fire truck coming down Kitten Creek Road. It pulled to a stop and waited to enter Anderson. Questions raced through our heads.

"Oh, Dear Lord, there must have been a fire on our road!"

"I wonder who? Where?'"

We were both speaking at the same time. I pressed my foot to the gas a little harder as we entered the gravel road and sped toward home. No more signs of fire trucks or activity. But as we got to the nearest neighbors, it became evident that the activity was in our own front yard.

"Oh, please, no, God!" I prayed softly.

As we pulled into the driveway, we took a quick inventory: the house was standing, the barn was still there. As another fire truck sped down the hillside out of the pasture, toward the barn and into the driveway, we realized that the fire must have been in the pasture. We Kansans do burn our pastures in the spring, but never, ever in the fall. With the wind and dry grasses, fall fires quickly grow out of control.

This fire *must* be stopped.

One truck remained in the pasture as we ventured up the hill to survey the damage. We walked across the black ashes and soot—all that remained of the grass. The volunteer firemen were still dousing the flames on the hillside above the prayer chapel. Not until we crawled down into the chapel, did we realize the extent of God's grace that day. The trucks had managed to get to the hillside just as the flames licked at the corner of the chapel. The only damage to the structure was where the fire had settled into a corner built of railroad ties and had smoldered there until the firemen reached it with hoses.

Later that evening, as Sara and Kay shared their experiences, we were able to piece together the story. The schools had been closed that afternoon for a half-day teacher in-service, and Sara, a middle-school student at that time, had been the only one at home. The rest of us were either at University or at work.

Arriving home on the bus after a morning of classes, Sara was relishing her freedom. She had settled in to a quiet reverie when the phone rang. Kay Bascom, our neighbor on the other side of the hill, was calling. "Sara ..." She paused. Not wanting to alarm Sara but very concerned, Kay chose her words carefully. "I think ... that maybe I am smelling smoke. Do you know if anyone is burning something?"

Sara, quick to hear the concern in Kay's voice, looked out the window. "No, I don't see anything," she said cautiously, "but let me go up in the pasture and check. I will call you back if I see anything."

Sara began to smell smoke as she climbed the hill, and then to see smoke—billows of smoke. A fire was coming from the south and raging toward the barn. Or so, at least, it appeared to her. Sara raced down the hill and into the house. Grabbing the phone, she dialed Kay's number. "Yes!" she reported breathlessly. "There *is* a fire, and it's headed our way!"

They quickly confirmed that Kay would call the fire department and Sara would call her dad. When Judd's secretary answered the phone and told Sara that Judd was in a session, Sara left a message: "The pasture is on fire and is headed toward the barn."

Meanwhile Kay had dialed 9-1-1 and the fire trucks were on their way. Knowing that the prayer chapel up in the ravine stood in the path of the flames, Kay got her water hose. Turning the water on full force, she stumbled up the path through the woods. But the hose was too short. Dropping the hose and scurrying back down to her home, out of breath and frantic, she grabbed two containers that would hold water, and ran back up the path. Filling each container, she valiantly ran back and forth to reach the chapel, wetting the outside walls. Finally she spied some men in black suits at the top of the hill looking down the ravine. "Help!" she shouted. "Please help me save this building!"

When the firemen arrived, they quickly assessed that the fire was not threatening the house and out buildings. However, on the hill above the barn, the fire was barreling its way across the pasture. Thinking that it was a simple pasture fire, the firemen were faithfully putting out the fire in the fields. Usually, fires that go down into the tree-filled ravines will burn themselves out, so they were not concerned about the fire that had reached the ravine where the prayer chapel was hidden from their view. Then, guided by Kay's directions, those volunteers got to the chapel just as the structure received its first licks from the flames. By the time Derrick and I arrived, the remaining fire truck with its crew were working to extinguish every last ember.

Now it has never been a secret that Kay does not appreciate the "pasture burning" process. In fact, Kay usually busies herself in town when a burn is planned. But this fateful day, Kay and Sara were the lone occupants of their respective homes. After that, Sara joined the ranks of pasture-burn naysayers.

A year later, our little community held a thanksgiving service down in that ravine. The chapel and the wooded hillside reverberated with the voices of our thankful group as Charles led us in singing, "Praise God from whom all blessings flow." Prayers were offered and scripture read. Beside the charred hole in the wood, a little bronze plaque was nailed that read, "Thou dost encompass me with deliverance" (Psalm 32:7). Yes, even when we are unaware of the dangers that may encompass us, he does prepare a way of deliverance: someone to smell the smoke, someone to put out the fire, a community of deliverers.

Leaving the chapel that day with a thankful group of friends, I turned to read the words inscribed above the chapel door, "Let him who is thirsty come; and whosoever will, let him take of the water of life freely" (Revelation 22:17). We were finding the sacred in the midst of the mundane.

SECTION TWO

The Gifts of Animals

13.
Blind Mama

I WAS MAKING MY WAY across the yard from the garden when I discerned a faint bleating sound floating down the hill from the pasture beyond. Listening for a response from the other sheep, I heard nothing. Blind Mama was in trouble again. The house had been my destination; but I turned instead to the hillside and made my way up the rocky path to the pasture. As I rounded the rise of the hill, on my right I could see the flock of sheep quite unconcernedly grazing in tall green prairie grass. The sound of the frantic bleating was coming from my left.

Poor Mama. She who had always been the leader of that currently unresponsive flock had headed blindly into a thicket. She was lost, totally. The rest of the sheep had found the grass and had seemingly tired of responding to her cries for help. At this point in her life, she was navigating the pasture by listening for the sounds of the rest of the flock.

As I untangled her from the thorns of the thicket, I remembered her early years. She was the first ewe we purchased.

We had met the Clacks at church and found we had much in common, one of those being the love of horses and wide open spaces. Anne and Bob invited us, a couple of their grown children, and a single neighbor lady, Diane, for a meal at their spacious ranch home. That evening the conversation around the dinner table slowly gravitated to our newly-acquired farm.

"We are looking for a couple of goats to help control the weeds all over the fields around the house," I said.

When Diane heard the words goat and weeds together, she became animated. "You don't want goats," she said. "What you need are some wooly weed eaters. I can guarantee they'll eat your weeds, they'll be easy to care for, and I can get you started." Diane had a little flock of sheep and obviously was a champion for the fine practice of raising sheep. "Besides, you can sell the wool. You would have an excellent product produced by your very own sheep."

It did not take long to convince me. Wanting to be a good neighbor, Judd agreed that sheep sounded good. His brother, Phil, had owned goats and was always getting in trouble with his neighbors over his wide-ranging, unstoppable goats.

Within a few days, we were the owners of a pregnant ewe. Little did Judd suspect that I would become captivated with being a "shepherdess" and eventually would acquire an entire flock.

"Blind Mama" was not her first name. In the beginning, I had quickly given her the distinguished name of Priscilla. Priscilla began the clean-up crew on our property; and she soon birthed a son, Aquila, shortened to Willy.

As my flock grew, Priscilla the old pro became the acknowledged leader of the flock. She would lead them up the hill to pasture, back for water, and to the safety of the barnyard for the night. They trusted her. She was wise, patient, and protective, particularly of her lambs.

Her eyesight had become worse and worse over time. Somehow, each pregnancy drew from her body the nourishment that her eyes required. With every new lamb that she "threw," I watched her cataracts grow thicker until finally her eyes were opaque.

Slowly her leadership became questionable. At first, I would find the entire flock packed against a corner of the pen, or wandering down into the dry bed of a stream. They would quietly stand, waiting for Priscilla to lead them out of the dilemma. I would go out and get Priscilla started in the right direction, rescuing her from her embarrassment. I don't know how long it took the flock to realize that she was leading them astray most of the time; but finally, a new leader took over.

This is the point where I began calling her Blind Mama. By now she was following the flock by listening to the sound of their movement; but when they stopped to graze, she would lose them. Hence, an effort to figure out where they were, she would constantly bleat. At first, several would respond to her. I could hear them calling back to her, and hear her responding until she was once again close to the rest of the sheep. Occasionally, however, they would leave her standing alone in the pasture as they came back to the barnyard for water or shade. Poor Mama.

Evidently, on this day, none of the flock was responding to her cries, and she was desperate. Time for me to find a new strategy. As I untangled her from the thicket and led her down to the barnyard, I devised a plan. I would be the leader. I would take them to pasture. Blind Mama would follow me, and the rest of the flock would follow Blind Mama.

In the beginning, I started with a little grain and a halter. She knew my voice, so I would talk to her. "Come Mama, come, Mama, here girl." Quickly she caught on. She would follow closely, listening to my voice and the rattle of the grain. Over a period of time, I no longer needed a halter or the grain. My voice was enough. Mama would put her nose against the back of my knee, and she would follow me wherever I led. The rest of the flock soon followed. We were now a team, Mama and I.

One evening I decided to switch them to different pasture. Instead of going down Kitten Creek Road, where traffic might be a safety factor, I decided to take them up across the pasture, down into the hardwood forest, along a ravine on a narrow path, and down into the pole shed pasture.

Mama and I led the way. "Come, girl, come, Mama," I repeated over and over as we made our way up the steep hill to the pasture. Sixteen sheep followed us. Mama, with her nose in the back of my knee was once more the leader. She had no idea where we were going; she did not even realize that she was in danger as we walked the narrow path of the ravine. Her faith was in me as she blindly followed, and the rest of the flock obediently trailed along.

That evening, I walked a parable with my sheep, and the lesson was imprinted in my soul. Just as Blind Mama in her disabilities could walk the paths and lead the rest of the flock, so can I lead. Not alone, but placing my confidence in the Shepherd.

14.
Peg

THE WEEDS AT THE FARM that needed to be cleared proved to be more than my first ewe, Priscilla, and her lamb, Aquila, could possibly eat by themselves. So we went back to the wooly weed-eater supplier, Diane, for our next pregnant ewe.

"Peg" was short for peg-leg, a descriptive name already given to this ewe because of her limp. Peg exhibited an independent spirit in her young life. Her shepherdess kept losing this wandering sheep. Not content with the pasture she had been offered, Peg was continually escaping the sheepfold.

One morning while Diane was eating breakfast, her phone rang. "Diane, that sheep of yours is over here in our pasture. Looks like she is headed for Anderson Avenue."

After thanking her farmer friend, she stepped out the door and gazed down the road. Sure enough, there was that wayward ewe. "She probably thinks she can find better grass than I provide," mused Diane. But Diane, her shepherd, saw the life-threatening danger, also.

Donning her jacket and grabbing a scoop of grain from the shed, Diane headed out, hoping to cajole Peg into coming back home. But Peg ignored her and instead wandered farther away.

The closer Diane got to her, the farther she wandered. Something had to be done or this silly sheep was in danger of losing her sheep life.

In desperation, Diane ran to the house. She grabbed her rifle then returned to the neighbor's field. Although the ewe's "sheep mind" could not have understood, it was out of affection that Diane, the shepherd, aimed carefully and shot Peg's leg.

Wounded, Peg fell to the ground. Finally able to approach her without Peg running away, Diane coaxed her to her feet. Peg had become docile. Bleeding and limping, she willingly followed her shepherdess back to the fold.

Peg's wound would heal in time, but she would always walk with a limp. Her limp would be a constant reminder to her, and to me her new owner, that although the lesson was a painful one, disobedience has consequences: a limp, but also a closer and more dependent relationship with the shepherd.

For Peg's own safety, her shepherd had had to wound her. Not because Diane did not care for her. Not because she was angry at her. Not because she was retaliating for her disobedience. Peg was wounded for her own safety and well being. Although it may not be exactly the same, it reminds me of Jacob wrestling with the angel. He also walked with a limp the rest of his life.

One frigid and icy New Year's morning, Peg and I bonded as shepherdess and docile sheep. An ice storm had hit on New Year's evening. Judd was gone on a retreat of solitude and silence, and Sara and I were holding down the fort. We woke up to at least an inch of ice covering the trees, grass, and road.

I had bundled up in my heavy-duty army jacket and pulled on the black insulated Air Force boots. With a wool hat pulled over my ears and warm work gloves covering my hands, I was prepared. Or at least I thought I was. It should have been a quick walk to the barn for grain, to the sheep pen for hay, and to the water tank to break up the ice and run some water.

My heavy boots slipped and slid across the icy yard and down the driveway to the barn. Bear, my black-lab "guardian of the barn," greeted me. I patted his head, filled his dish with some kibbles, and refilled his water bowl. Scooping up the grain for the sheep from the bin, I headed back out into the icy yard.

By this time, the sheep knew I was coming. They shoved and pushed each other in an effort to get close to their breakfast. All except one! Peg had not shown up. I dumped the grain into the feeder. My eyes scanned the large pen. Up against the fence at the top of the hill stood a gray wooly bundle. This was not good.

"Hey, Peg," I called to her. She lifted her head to look but didn't budge. She slowly lowered her head and became a wooly bundle again.

I studied the situation for a minute and decided I had to get closer to her and evaluate what was going on; but in these freezing temperatures, the hillside was nearly impossible to climb. The west fence would be my tow rope up the icy slope, I decided.

All was stillness. Ice sparkled on the trees, leaves, and fence. Under other circumstance I would be mesmerized by the splendor of the scene; but at this moment my focus was on my obviously-suffering ewe.

As I neared the ewe, I discovered she was in labor and having great difficulty. The lamb's nose and one leg were visible ... but only *one* leg! For easy lambing the head should lie between the two front legs. Peg was in trouble. Push as hard as she could, she was not going to get this lamb dislodged.

Back down the hill I slid to call Dr. Penner, our farm vet who had already walked with me through some farm crises. Peg and I needed help. My phone call got through to Dr. Penner at a garage in town where he was waiting for a tire to be changed. As icy as the roads were, I knew it would take him some time to get here, even after the tire was fixed. I grabbed towels, pulled on snow pants, warmed my hands by the wood stove, and hurried back to Peg.

Once again I climbed the hill using the fence for assistance. Peg was resting when I reached her. Sitting down on the ice beside her, I began praying. "God, you are my shepherd, and I don't know how to help my sheep. She is your creature also. Please help us."

A song came to mind and I began to sing it softly to her, trying to comfort both of us.

> *Beside the still waters in pastures of green,*
> *The Shepherd is leading where all is serene;*
> *By day and by night He will always be seen*
> *Beside the still waters of peace.*
> *For He's the Good Shepherd who died for the sheep;*
> *His own He has promised to keep.*
> *He lovingly watches and guards while they sleep*
> *Beside the still waters of peace.*

The song comforted me as I imagined my Shepherd, and our Creator, there with us. We weren't exactly in green pastures and beside still water; but he was lovingly watching and guarding us.

My voice seemed to comfort Peg for awhile. Then she

returned to her fruitless pushing. About an hour since I had called Dr. Penner I was at a loss, straining my ears for the sound of a vehicle coming down Kitten Creek Road. No traffic sounds at all. Maybe the doc wouldn't even be able to get here on these icy roads.

Then Peg flopped her head down on the ground and appeared to stop breathing.

"She is dying! I am going to lose them both! Oh, dear God, I don't know what to do. But I've got to do something. Please help me."

With that, I pulled off my gloves, rolled up my sleeve, and reached inside where I had seen a leg. Never before had I had an experience like this, but I was going to do whatever I could. If I didn't try, she would die for sure, and so would the lamb. Amazingly, I found another leg turned under and apparently making it impossible for Peg to push out the lamb. Carefully, I straightened the leg and gave a tug. Out came a wet little lamb.

Peg lay there oblivious. Grabbing the lamb I carried it to her nose. "Look, Mama. Look at what we have done," I squealed. Peg raised her head, alert now. Giving a motherly, low and soft *meh*, she began licking and nudging her newborn. A few seconds later, she began pushing again. Out popped another lamb as easily as you please.

I was ecstatic!

However, now we had two very wet and cold little lambs. I had to get them safely down to the warmth of the barn. Holding the lambs near Peg's face, I encouraged her to stand. Slowly she crawled to her feet. Wrapping the lambs in the towels I had brought from the house, the four of us crept down the icy, slick hill.

Just as I reached the bottom, Dr. Penner drove up to the barn. Climbing out and shutting the door to his van, he chortled, "You did it! All by yourself! Congratulations."

After examining the lambs and their mother, and bedding them down in dry straw, we trudged to the van together, ice crunching as we walked. Dr. Penner had always seemed to understand my love for my sheep. "They are going to be fine, Nancy, and so are you," he said with a proud smile.

I didn't explain to him that I hadn't done it alone. But I was keenly aware that my Shepherd had been there with me the whole time.

15.
A Wool Story

WE WERE IN THE MIDST of a great struggle. With my knees deep in loose straw, I knelt in the dusty barn, struggling to contain two frantic lambs, one under each arm. Under the glaring light bulb, about fifteen feet from us, another struggle was ensuing, and the lambs were distressed. From their perspective it was a life-and-death struggle. The mother, who was under the spotlight, had experienced this indignity before, but she was distressed over her lambs' distress.

The temperature in the old barn was uncomfortably warm, and the large young man, shearing the ewe, dripped with perspiration as he wrestled to keep her still. The piles of wool grew with each swath he carved through her deep winter blanket. Spring had blossomed; for her comfort this was necessary. The wool must come off.

The stone walls reverberated with bleating from the frantic lambs, replies from their concerned mother, and loud droning of the electric shears. These three sheep, mother and twins, formed a tight-knit threesome. An excellent mother, she constantly called them back when they bounded too far from the rest of the flock.

As I watched the concerned ewe, I remembered the time

I had taken the flock out of the enclosed pen to allow them some grazing time in the orchard. The two lambs, inquisitive and unaware of any danger, had left the flock and their mother for "greener pastures" and had crossed the gravel road.

Mother Priscilla (all my sheep had names), saw them cross and also saw a pick-up barreling down the road toward them. Her frantic calls to the lambs went unheeded, and in desperation she ran in front of the truck. Fortunately, Jerry, our farmer friend on the north, had seen the drama unfolding and was slowing down ... not quickly enough to miss the mama, but enough to miss the lambs. As Priscilla picked herself up from the road we saw a big gash in her chest, but her only concern was to get those wayward lambs back on the right side of the road.

On shearing day, in the dusty barn, her concern was still for the lambs. Loudly bleating to them, struggling to extract her head from the tight grip of the shearer so she could see them, she tried to reassure them she was surviving the indignities of this ordeal. Finally, when my arms could hardly restrain the wriggling bodies any longer, the shearer released Priscilla. Scrambling to her feet she ran to a safe corner of the barn, calling her babies to come to her. As I released them, I fully expected them to dart to her side.

What happened next gave me great pause for reflection. Instead of running to Mama, they bounded to the large heap of wool. Nosing it, walking around it, they became even more distressed. Where had she gone? This is the wool we remember. But it is silent now. It has been emptied of life. Getting up and dusting off my knees, I went over to the pile of wool and carefully bundled up the lambs again. As I placed them beside the shorn-naked mother, her familiar voice began to soothe their anxieties and once again they found contentment in the comfort of her familiar presence.

My lifelong questions seem to haunt me. What is God doing? Where is he going? And sometimes: where has he gone? My heart resonates with the cry of the Psalmist: "I would have despaired unless I had believed that I would see the hand of the Lord in the land of the living" (Psalm 27:13).

I am excited when I see God at work. There is a euphoria about it. Sometimes I see his footstep leading a new way, and a sense of adventure arises in my soul. But there is a hidden danger in this process of following God. As soon as I become attached to the place where I think he is, as soon as I get comfortable in my relationship to him, I begin to settle in and, without realizing it, get attached to the stuff—the ritual, the feelings—that comes with the obedience of following him. How long does it take me to awaken to the fact that these things are not the relationship? Instead of the adventure of following and obeying him, I find myself trying to protect and defend the "stuff."

Lately, though, I have been wrestling with an inarticulate longing. When I look around at my "place" in this whirling globe, I find myself grappling with questions, more questions than answers. I rely on the Holy Spirit to unveil the meanings behind the news, behind the scripture, and then, how that touches my own simple life here on Kitten Creek. His promises become my security for today, for the moment. I desperately need to see "his hand" in this land of the living. His presence is here, in this fallen world, and I will continue to "wait for the Lord and let my heart take courage" (Psalm 27:14).

However, how often in my life have I run to the wool? The wool of a community that had nurtured my wobbling faith in my teens. The wool of songs that had encouraged my heart as I grew in my faith and expressed my love and devotion to my Father. The wool of the farm where I had found my niche, a canvas of so many possibilities to create ministry and offer hospitality.

Yet he has never left. He continues to call my attention to himself, and after I have mourned over my pile of wool, with the nudging of his Spirit I find him again and again.

16.
Lessons In Lambing

THE CLOCK ON MY DRESSER showed two o'clock a.m. I reached for my old red bathrobe draped by the bed and sleepily made my way to the back door. Stepping into my mud boots and warm jacket, I grabbed a flashlight and slipped out into the cool night air. With each step I took, I could feel my bathrobe softly wrap around my bare legs. Turning sleep-hungry eyes toward the starlit sky I whispered, "So, God, what lesson am I learning … or supposed to learn … through this new adventure?" Getting up every two hours should have some reward, I reasoned. Maybe it will be twins … two prize ewes or grand champion rams. I was confident God would reward me for the sleep-deprived nights.

My Good Shepherd doesn't always respond in a voice that I can discern with my earthly ears, but I know that he tenderly loves this slow-witted sheep of his and works everything for good. So through the chilly night I expectantly made my way toward the dark barn.

Our old black lab, Bear, had become so familiar with my vigilance, that he was no longer shocked into wakefulness every time I entered the barn. He simply blinked and thumped his tail against the straw bed in a doggy greeting as my light beam flashed across his face in search of the ewe.

There she stood, contentedly munching away at the pile of hay I had given her earlier. This was not a hopeful sign … ewes in labor do not eat. However, she was young, barely a year, so perhaps she was not aware of what ewes do when they are in labor. I resumed my now-familiar position on a bale of hay, trying not to disturb her from any labor pains which might be in progress

The night noises enveloped me. I could hear the rest of the flock just outside. A ewe softly called her lamb back to her side. One lone neighbor dog barked in the distance. My attention shifted back inside the barn where I listened to Josephine chewing her cud and Bear softly snoring. After fifteen minutes of watching a sheep getting nervous about being watched, I headed back to the house.

I could have been sleeping. This was a wasted trip. I crawled back into my warm bed beside my peacefully sleeping husband.

Two weeks earlier Josephine, one of my lambs from the previous year, had begun a pregnancy prolapse. So I had made a quick call to our faithful vet, and then began the now-familiar routine of catching the sheep, holding her while the birth canal was sewn shut, rubbing her face and trying to convince her this was for her own good. The year before, I had held her half-sister's head and stroked her face as the same vet had given her a shot to ease her death. She too had prolapsed, but we had not caught her until the entire uterus and lamb had been partially expelled along with part of her bowels. A tough experience for the ewe, for me, and even for the vet. I did not want to see another ewe encounter that agony.

Although he knew I needed no reminder, Doc Penner gave me off-handed instructions as he drove away. "Keep an eye on her! You've got to get those stitches out as soon as she goes into labor …" He did not need to finish his warning: "or you will lose the lamb and the ewe," was the obvious conclusion.

And so began my careful monitoring of Josephine's behavior. To begin, I built a pen for her in the barn. Comfortable straw for bedding, fresh hay to eat, her own feed bucket, a pail of water. Josephine had been one of my most optimistic, social, and energetic lambs. In the large sheep pen, she was the one who always came running first to check for grain—or just a simple cheek rub, which was reward enough. Josephine's social spirit made her agonizingly aware of her solitary confinement; so, thinking this could be a matter of hours, possibly days, I brought her mother into the barn to keep her company.

I had entered the project with enthusiasm. But the days dragged on … and on … and on. Every two to three hours became a routine that affected everything I did. I would leave school (I was teaching full time at our local Christian college which was about twenty minutes from the farm) to go home and check the sheep. I had to be close enough to the farm that I could always be available. And those nights! I had asked God to wake me up so I would not have to set an alarm and wake Judd. He was faithful; so I always tried to be obedient and respectful of his faithfulness. I had it down to a science: look at the clock; sit up quietly; ease the blankets back so Judd would stay warm; tip-toe out of the room. I was learning plenty. This whole routine of waking, getting out of bed, and showing consideration for my husband, was teaching me self discipline, faith, and obedience.

Three weeks after we began our labor watch, Josephine began to push. This is it! Now we will see what it is you are carrying in that large tummy. Intruding into her life, I caught her, held her down, and pulled out the stitches. Offended by my actions, she retreated from me, not understanding in the least my verbal explanation of what I was doing and why. But … nothing happened, except another prolapse, another embarrassed call to the vet, another escapade of catching, holding, sewing.

It would be another two weeks before Josephine became a mother. Two more weeks of waking, or of driving home from school, sitting quietly on my bale of hay. Finally, she delivered a nice little ewe lamb. Not twins, nothing spectacular, but a sweet ewe lamb. And Josephine was a good mother, sharing her one lamb with her twin sister who had lost hers and desperately wanted to be a mother. The three of them ran around in the barnyard together, both moms watching out for their precious charge. A threesome! That new little lamb not only had me, her shepherdess, but constant care from two mothers.

Yes, my threesome was fun to observe out in the corral. But more than that I recall with joy the many starlit nights of quiet worship as I walked to the barn, the trips home to a peaceful farm, the knowledge that I had a God who cared about this sheep of his and yet also cared for my sheep, a God who would faithfully walk with me through this experience, waking me from my both literal and metaphorical sleep, to see his hand mysteriously working in the land of the living.

17.
FROM THE MOUTH OF A DONKEY?

I PLACED THE HOT CUP of coffee on the end table, sank down into the brown recliner, and opened my worn Bible. This was my routine: rising while the house was still quiet and before the sun had lightened the sky, filling my coffee cup, and settling in for my daily soul check. Once it was daylight, I would don my worn barn jacket, pull on my boots and go out to the barnyard to do the chores. After the animals were fed and I had eaten breakfast, I would dress in my more presentable school clothes and head off to the college for another day of books and students and papers. But this quietness here in the near-morning, this solitude … this was *my* time.

The passage in II Peter 2 was quite alarming, yet I had to admit that I recognized those "false prophets" in our world today: those who indulge in the flesh, self-willed, reveling in the day time, forsaking the right way. And then as I read, my mind switched from thinking about this fallen world to thinking about my life on the farm: "Forsaking the right way they have gone astray, having followed the way of Balaam, the son of Beor, who loved the wages of unrighteousness, but he received a rebuke for his own transgression; for a dumb donkey, speaking with a voice of a man, restrained the madness of the prophet."

My mind turned from the dire warning of false prophets and the fallen world in which I lived to my more immediate world on Kitten Creek Road. I giggled to myself. God can even make a dumb donkey talk. Am I surprised? My miniature donkey, Sandino, had a character all his own. He also had several important jobs. For most of the year, he was protector of my small flock of sheep. Our pastures and farm were surrounded by packs of coyotes that we could hear howling in the distance in the evenings. I had witnessed Sandino chasing stray dogs out of the pasture with his head down and his teeth bared. No predator was safe, and the sheep were secure. In the Fourth of July Keats parade, Sandino proudly carried small children on his back. The little village just at the end of Kitten Creek Road, celebrated with a nostalgic hometown parade every Independence Day. Along with the local high school band, the volunteer fire truck, trusty old tractors, and restored cars from the 1950s, Sandino carried his charges with pride. But his most important jobs boasted of a more sacramental nature.

At two separate events every year Sandino was given a major role in our production of Bethlehem Revisited, the walk-through drama held here on the farm in December. Thirteen times a night, three evenings in a row, led by Joseph and carrying a pregnant Mary, Sandino patiently marched up to the Inn, each time to discover that there was "no room." He was more than a stock character; he reveled in his role.

His second role was to carry Jesus into a crowded church in Clay Center, a nearby town, on Palm Sunday. Every year our friend Char would call and book Sandino for that particular weekend. It seemed that the whole church looked forward to his participation in the celebration of Jesus' ride into Jerusalem. Never once did he misbehave or disturb the sanctity of the church, as he walked down the aisle carrying a humble Christ on his back. In all of his roles he was a gentleman who seemed to recognize the importance of having a good presence.

When my devotions were completed, I headed to the back door and pulled on my chore coat, a worn, heavy army jacket. Far from being stylish or feminine, it was warm, had deep pockets, a good zipper, and worked perfectly for cold winter chores. As I headed across the yard I patted the empty, right pocket and remembered that I had somehow misplaced the paring knife when doing the evening chores the night before. That knife was an important part of my work routine. With it I could easily cut open the next bale of hay, open bags of feed, or cut string to tie up an opening in a gate or fence. That knife was my main chore tool. But it was gone, and could be gone forever under loose hay if I did not find it quickly. As I walked, my mind ran through the possibilities of where that knife could be and how I might ever find it.

Usually, as I opened bales, I would pull off a couple of flakes and toss them out to the animals. The knife could be between the bales, on top of one of the bales, or worse yet, it could be under loose hay, sinking deeper with every movement the animals made as they trampled through the shed. I needed that knife, but truth be told, I was doubtful I would be successful in finding it. I lifted up my request once more to the God who sees all things and can help me find all things if he so chooses. (This statement comes from a gal who is prone to losing things.)

Halfway across the yard I noticed that Sandino was not at the gate waiting for me. All the sheep were waiting expectantly at the fence; but no donkey. Usually, Sandino, hearing the screen door slam, knew this meant I was on my way. I would find him at the gate braying his morning greeting. But today no Sandino appeared. Concerned, I began to call to him while I continued my way across the bottom yard. When I stepped up to the gate, as if on cue from one of his performances, that little donkey trotted out from the shed. Running up to the gate where I was standing, he skidded to a halt, dropped my precious paring knife at my feet, and exclaimed with a loudly exultant bray!

I stood there in great disbelief and amusement. Yes, God can use a donkey in miraculous ways ... even today. Somehow my morning devotions became even more complete than what I had expected. Only God could have orchestrated that morning. So what is the meaning of this experience? An object lesson? A sense of humor? I am not sure. I love the thought that God is involved in our daily existence. Perhaps that is the only lesson that he was writing in my life that day. He uses the mundane, the earthy, and the unimpressive to bring astonishment, joy, humor into our lives. I am not sure I need a message any deeper than "Yes, I, your Lord God, am here, walking with you across the barnyard, sitting with you at your desk, eating with you in the kitchen. Even laughing with you. I will never leave you nor forsake you." Expecting the unexpected is part of the excitement and joy of living with an eye to see God in our everyday lives.

18.
My "Hey, Sheep"

REX WAS GONE. After several long weeks of incapacitating weakness, my "Hey, Sheep" had finally died.

Rex, his given name, had come to live at the farm to be a companion to Arabella, the "defective" ewe that was living out the rest of her life on the farm. Rex was a big sheep, well over two-hundred pounds. I was the one person who could approach him without fearing his ram-like aggression. Supposedly a wether when we bought him, we slowly discovered (there must be a biblical axiom "you can judge a ram by his fruits") that he had never been totally stripped of all his male accoutrements. No one who had been knocked down by Rex would vouch for the success of that de-ramming. In fact the last shearer had found his "ramness" too much to wrestle to make it worth another shearing, and had carried bruises for over a week.

Every summer after that shearing fiasco, I took pity on him. My father-in-law had purchased a pair of hand shears for me, so on a particularly hot day I would dig out those old shears and head for the sheep pen. Sitting on the bench of a picnic table with Rex's collar tightly held in my left hand, I would snip away at the deep, thick coat of wool. He seemed to enjoy those interludes of my undivided attention. My shearing attempts went only as far as Rex would allow me to go, which meant that I could do his back and sides, but definitely not his belly. Thus, every summer, when all the other neighboring sheep ran around trim and clean, Rex sported a long skirt that hung from his midsection to the ground. He never had to suffer the humiliation of the other sheep who had been stripped naked. At least that seemed to suffice as an excuse when other sheep owners raised their eyebrows at my shearing expertise.

After Arabella died, I put our miniature donkey, Sandino, in the sheep pen with Rex. Rex greeted this companion with bruising and ramming. In desperation I let him run with the two horses for a day, thinking they would intimidate him into submission and gentleness, but I quickly decided I might have some serious vet bills to pay if the horses continued in the same vicinity as Rex. So Rex became master of his own domain—lonely, but in control.

He also had lost all invitations to be a part of our living nativity. Every year we host about two-thousand people who walk through the guided tour of what we call Bethlehem Revisited. After I sold my flock of sheep, we trailered in a flock from Kansas State. We had tried Rex as part of the borrowed flock joining the shepherds "out in the fields." Not a joiner, however, he was quickly rejected from that role. Next, we tried tying him at the manger with Mary, Joseph, and baby Jesus. Tied far enough away that he could not harm the sleeping baby, unfortunately he was close enough to carefully gauge a sneaky jab at the back of the magi's knee which sent the unsuspecting wiseman solidly to the ground. So, once again Rex became just background noise with his occasional unique "baa" (which sounded more like a rumbling, deep burp) as the group walked past his pen.

It was after ostracizing him to a distant pen that I began to call him "Hey, Sheep." In the mornings and evenings as I exited the kitchen door to do my feeding chores, Rex would begin to call to me. And I would respond, "Hey, Sheep." It became our little ritual. After months and years of doing this, I almost forgot that his name was Rex.

And now, after years of residency on the farm, "Hey Sheep" was beginning to falter. He had long passed the age that most sheep live. For weeks he hadn't been able to stand for long, and when he fell could not get up without help. I would tug and pull on his wooly, 200-plus pound body, lifting him up until he could get his feet planted securely under himself. As he wobbled to find his balance, I would slowly walk away hoping that this time he would gather the strength he needed to keep going.

I gave him glucosamine, tried to make his pen free from anything that would trip him, and held my breath, waiting for him to get better. Each morning when, after getting him stabilized the night before, I went out to feed the other animals I would find him lying helplessly on his side. As soon as he heard my voice, he would begin to struggle to get to his feet, his legs striking the air in frantic movements. And once again I would go to his pen and struggle to get his feet planted back on the ground.

My energy dipped, and my anticipation each morning began to be replaced with a heavy sense of dread. Coming around the side of the barn I would let my gaze sweep to the far south of the barnyard, up the slight hill of the sheep pen, and fall upon (oh, blast it!) the wooly, white mound with legs pumping fruitlessly against the air.

I finally decided to let nature take its course. I knew that animals, particularly sheep and horses, cannot survive if they don't get up. I felt that maybe it was my encouragement that kept him alive. Maybe, if he did not hear my voice, he would give up and die. Maybe that would be less cruel than keeping him alive. So ... for two days I whispered when I was outside so he could not hear my voice. When I fed the other animals, I stayed far away from the sheep pen. Yes, he was down. No, he was not moving.

The morning of the third day I worked up the courage to go to his pen. Slowly walking up to his body, I whispered, "Hey Sheep." To my dismay, his legs began pumping and he threw back his head to look for me.

I have always felt that one of my strongest callings has been to be a caretaker of God's creatures. It is a deep-down kind of calling that, were I to turn my back on it, I would be denying a huge part of my very essence, something that has defined my soul. So when I am faced with failure in that caretaking, when I bump up against this fallen world that faces the curse of death, I am forced to recognize that we are not home yet. Nor are our animals. We are all suffering from that fateful act of disobedience in the garden.

Not able to watch my sheep go through any more suffering, I finally called our country vet. I led her to where Rex lay and watched as she listened to his heart (fine and strong), his breathing (regular, lungs clear). No problems there, but obviously he would not survive long in his prone condition. I thankfully watched as she administered the shot that would ease him into oblivion.

As we walked away from his limp body, finally at rest, I mourned the loss of another one of my friends and I recalled a plaque that my mother had bought for me when I was a teen-ager:

> The friends of my childhood
> Were mostly stray cats,
> Or poor homeless dogs
> All forlorn.
>
> I wonder where now
> Are their dim trusting souls,
> Those friends whom
> I still faintly mourn.

To the list of my cats and dogs, I have added sheep, horses, donkeys, cows, and now a goat—all my friends.

I like the picture that C.S. Lewis paints in *The Great Divorce* when he portrays a character named Sarah Smith from Golders Green. Lewis gives us his own attempt at trying to understand the role that human beings may have as caretakers of God's creatures. In *The Great Divorce*, the narrator is being guided through the foothills of heaven by his old mentor, George MacDonald, when wonderful expectation fills the air. A procession of joyful bright spirits comes out of the distance, followed by boys and girls singing, all preceding a lady in whose honor all this is being done. Her face shines with unbearable beauty. The narrator relates that following the lovely lady were cats, "dozens of cats. And all those dogs ... why, I can't count them. And the birds. And the horses."

When the narrator queries his guide, MacDonald explains:

> They are her beasts. ... Every beast and bird that came
> near her had its place in her love. In her they became

themselves. And now the abundance of life she has in Christ from the Father flows over into them. … It is like when you throw a stone into a pool, and the concentric waves spread out further and further. Who knows where it will end?

Hey Sheep had his own quirky, cantankerous personality. But he was one of God's creatures, and I had become his devoted caretaker. With that caretaking came responsibility, but also joy and, in a sense, worship of the Creator who had placed him here in this little patch of farmland that I call home.

Section Three

The Gifts that Keep On Giving

19.
A Barn? Or The Longest Covered Bridge In Kansas?

"WATER DEEP," A CHRISTIAN FOLK BAND from Kansas City, stepped up on the wagon and took their mics. "Good evening, everyone!"

We sat on benches placed in semi circles around the hay wagon, now a stage, with amps, microphones, and instruments. My eyes wandered to the horizon. The sun, going down behind us, painted the eastern sky with a pink and blue reflection. Joy of working together was written on the faces of the group that was gathered on that hillside.

I sat beside Judd, sensing the exhilaration he was feeling, though I also noticed a little apprehension clouding his eyes as he listened to the young people singing along with the band.

Judd leaned over and whispered, "You know, I had one thought as we walked past that barn tonight: tomorrow that may still be a barn, or it may be the longest covered bridge in Kansas."

I smiled, admitting the barn did look a little crazy. Both ends were standing open to the wind. Earlier today, on forty- and twenty-foot scaffolds young people had been climbing, ripping out nails, pulling the long barn boards off, and tossing them to the ground. Another crew was pulling what nails were still in the boards, and stacking them carefully on a pile. While some were taking care of the old barn wood, others were painting the new boards that would replace the old.

Tonight we were celebrating the accomplishments of this day. Before our eyes, a barn was being transformed. Hopefully, by evening tomorrow the work would be completed; but tonight was a time of anticipation and thanksgiving.

The project had been carefully orchestrated and was overseen by one man. He called it "Nehemiah (Nineteen) Ninety Five." Following Nehemiah's example, we were building walls—barn walls, that is.

Darrel had formulated the plan earlier in the spring as the Junior High camp weekend had been winding down. The camp was called "Fannin' the Flame." It was his vision to bring junior-high youth from various churches in Manhattan out to the farm. Tents were erected with the boys' camp at one end of the pasture and the girls' at the other.

With the help of two young couples from our church, Darrel had managed to pull off an impressive, life-changing weekend for these young teens.

Saturday afternoon parents gradually arrived to take the young people home. All that was left was the clean-up. Darrel sat gazing at the barn and all around. "What a great place," he commented. "It has been perfect for this type of camp. I think I would like to do it again next year, if you will let us." There was a question in his statement.

"Of course!" Judd and I spoke as one. We loved having the farm used in this manner. We loved the young people. We loved to see people with a vision for ministry.

Darrel is probably one of the most energetic, enthusiastic,

and positive men I have ever met. I am sure he had already been thinking about his next idea before he spoke. On the other hand, Darrel was also quite a spontaneous individual, so what came out of his mouth next, may or may not have been planned.

"Some of the slats on your east and west sides are in bad shape, Judd. I have a proposal." With that, he began to rattle Judd's cage. "We can have an old-fashioned barn raising! In one weekend, we can tear off both sides of the barn, replace them, and paint the rest of the barn."

Our barn still sported a faint, half-century-old paint job. It was definitely more *old* than red. It could use a good coat of paint, just as it could use new barn wood. But, in a weekend?

Judd hesitated. If things went wrong, we would be in serious trouble. "No, no, that's alright. We can do it ourselves. Some-time."

But Darrell persisted. "Look, I have organized missions projects and we have built houses in a week. I can get this done."

"I'll have to think about it," came Judd's cautious response.

After a week or more of discussion and persuasion, Judd finally relented. "OK, I'll turn it over to you."

Darrell and his team got busy.

Thus, here we were, celebrating. Darrell had contacted Christian groups on K-State campus who had used the barn over the years for their barn parties; he went to a local lumber store to ask for donations of wood; arranged for the local radio station to come and cover the project; invited Water Deep for a concert in the pasture. Food, paint, electrical supplies, and anything else that could be desired, seemed to be provided. Besides working on the barn, there were men building a loft in the granary which had become my *Poustinia* cabin, a place for those who wanted to get away for silence and solitude. It seemed that we were the recipients of more than an old-fashioned barn raising.

The area around the barn resembled a busy ant farm: people painting new boards, people pulling nails, people working on the cabin, people climbing to dangerous heights on the scaffolding, people manning the radio-station broadcasting from inside the torn-up barn. Finally, when new groups kept coming, I pulled a few people aside and said, "I think one of our greatest needs right now is for someone to circle the barn praying for safety." I don't know how many pray-ers we actually had, but it made me feel better.

One of the reasons we had bought the farm in the first place was because of the grand old barn. Stacked to the high rafters with old hay, we could envision it cleaned and usable for much more than storing hay. A solid stone foundation below the hay housed what had been the old milking barn with stanchions and troughs on one side and what had perhaps been calving pens on the other side. Through the years this part of the barn would be storage, a sheep pen, a goat pen, or whatever else needed housing.

The barn, along with the rest of the farm, was God's. We were stewards of this gift, and it seems God had many plans for what was his.

Beginning with the Spiritual Dynamics Conference, to the Family Conferences and the Creativity Conferences we hosted, there were also barn parties hosted by Christian groups from Kansas State University. With a short list of requirements—loud music must end by 11:30, no alcohol, no smoking, clean-up and turn lights out before leaving—the groups had free reins for their parties. There was no charge, except that they ask their members to volunteer for our work days.

"Are you related to the Swihart barn?" is a question we hear often as we introduce ourselves to people we meet across the country who have fond memories of what they experienced at the barn.

One Saturday evening at our regular Wellspring meeting, Carol R. dropped a startling question. It sounded like she said, "Would it be possible to have a dying party at the barn?"

Visions of caskets and sack cloth emerged in my mind. "A dying party? How would you do that?" I murmured.

"I am in a spinning and wool dyeing club," Carol explained. "We could bring our wool, vats, and drying racks, go out and gather flowers and leaves and weeds from the pasture, then share the experience of dyeing wool the natural way. The women would love this!"

So, now we can boast of having had a "dying" party in the barn.

For a few years, a very popular activity offered in the barn was a "coffeehouse experience." The idea had been born within the Wellspring group. Why? We loved coffee; we loved music; we loved the barn. Why not put it all together and have a party? We found a group of people who played classical string music, decorated the barn with tables donned in colorful cloths, found games that we scattered around on the tables, rounded up some espresso machines, made baked goods, and voilà! We had the makings of a coffeehouse. The evening was fantastic—or so we thought.

It turned out that some young people who were invited to the coffeehouse thought otherwise.

At school the following week, I was approached by one of my students who had attended our coffeehouse. Forming his thoughts carefully, Rustin offered his opinion, "Mrs. Swihart, that was not really a coffeehouse, at least not what young people would call a coffeehouse." Then he made an offer that was to change the dynamics in the barn for several years. "If you will let us, Satellite Soul will plan the coffeehouse evenings."

Satellite Soul, a local Christian band that Rustin played in, were excellent musicians who deeply desired to serve God and know him better. Rustin was already involved in Wellspring. Tim Suttle, Satellite Soul's leader, later joined our group. Rustin attended Manhattan Christian College, and Tim attended K-State, and both were active in the college-town culture. (Today, both Tim and Rustin are in the pastoral ministry.)

Even though we had had fun doing our idea of a coffeehouse, evidently it was time for the younger generation to take over. And they did. Once a month in the fall we had what they called "Coffeehouse at the Barn." Besides their own band, they also invited other Christian bands from the state. They advertised, they brought their equipment, and they rocked the barn. As a result, hundreds of young college students and high school students enjoyed an evening on the farm.

The music was loud enough to entertain all of Keats, a very small town. The people of Keats were probably glad it only occurred once a month!

One evening I stood near the coffee bar watching the young people: some were seated at a table playing cards; two sat at another table deeply engaged in a chess match; some were sitting back enjoying the music and sipping their coffee. Several sauntered in the double-door entrance to the barn, and one young man walked over to me. He stood awhile, observing and listening. Finally, above the deafening sounds of the band, he shouted, "This is wonderful!"

I smiled and nodded.

"Do you do anything else here besides the coffeehouse?" he asked.

I got close to his ear and shouted back, "Yes! We have retreats of silence."

He reacted with a questioning look of surprise; then he smiled.

It was true. Although the barn was a central part of ministry at the farm, we also offered another, very different kind of hospitality.

20.
A Poustinia Experience

SOME DEAR FRIENDS OF OURS from California moved to Colorado about the same time we moved to Kansas. Judd and "A" (I'll use this couple's initials) had served together on the staff of a large church in California. They had bonded through some difficult situations at the church. Colorado and Kansas are in fairly close proximity, so they and their children had come to visit us.

Somehow we always managed to find room in our tiny little farmhouse for guests. We gave the couple our bedroom, and their small sons slept on the floor. Their two teen-age girls slept on the fold-out couch in the living room. That many people—our three children and the two of us along with a family of six—in one small cottage may sound unpleasant. But truly, we treasured the time. And I treasure the memory, because it was during their visit that I discovered what was to become my passion.

As usual when we had guests, we had a "farm breakfast." As we sat around the table visiting, our conversation drifted to what further dreams we had for this new venture in our lives. It was obvious to these friends how much we loved our new existence. "B"—who is an avid reader—looked directly at me and asked, "Have you ever thought of having a *Poustinia?*"

"A *what?*" I had never even heard the word before.

She spelled the word and then explained. "I have been reading a book by a Russian Orthodox Christian, Catherine deHuek Doherty, who immigrated to America in the early 1900s. She has established *Poustinias* across this continent."

"What exactly is a *Poustinia?*" I was intrigued.

Like myself, my friend has a penchant for the spiritual disciplines of silence and solitude, and was very enthusiastic about her new reading adventure. "It is just a simple cabin where a person can go to be alone with God. You have the space here. You could have *Poustinia* cabins here."

After our guests left, I began my search for the book, that was published in 1975. The Christian bookstore in Manhattan did not carry it, but ordered it for me. *Poustinia: Christian Spirituality of the East for the Western Man* became my guidebook for establishing what I called retreats of silence and solitude. Our bookstore had to order more copies as I shared my new-found passion. Along with Willard's book, *The Spirit of the Disciplines*, Foster's books on spiritual disciplines, and Henri Nouwen, Doherty became another of my spiritual mentors. More were to follow as I lived out my passion.

When we first moved to the farm, the solitude and silence of walking among God's creation had brought healing to my soul. When I read Doherty's work, even though she wrote from a very Orthodox position, I found my heart resonating with her. In encouraging silence and solitude she writes:

How can one really achieve solitude? By standing still. Stand still, and allow the strange, deadly restlessness of our tragic age to fall away like the worn-out dusty cloak that it is—a cloak that was once considered beautiful. The restlessness was considered the magic carpet to tomorrow, but now in reality we see it for what it is: a running away from oneself, a turning from that journey inward that all men must undertake to meet God dwelling with the depths of their souls.

Poustinia means a quiet, lonely place where people can go to spend time with God. For Doherty, all a *Poustinia* should contain was a table, a chair, a bed, and a Bible—very simple.

We already had two cabins on the property. One was the old granary which we had swept out, washed the walls, and put in bunks. Another was the cabin built out of old hog sheds and chicken sheds. The Bascom sons had built this cabin up on the hill behind the farmhouse. That cabin was creatively established, planned as they went, dependent upon scavenged materials. The view from the front porch offered a peaceful scene of the fields across the road. When Charles and Kay Bascom built their log home, Kay called their basement apartment *Poustinia*. Theirs was the most civilized, since it had all the conveniences of home: shower, toilet, electricity, and running water.

The last cabin we added was built by our son Dan with Judd's help. Dan's vision was to build a place where our pastor, or anyone who was wanting to get away from phones and be alone, could go for a time of solitude, prayer, and study. After cutting down cedars in the back woods about a half mile from the house, they took them to a mill, had them planed and dried, and built a tiny cabin in a small clearing. This isolated cabin is probably our best example of Doherty's idea of a *Poustinia*. Many pastors and others have made their way to that cabin.

Over the years these *Poustinia* cabins have been used, sometimes by a single person who desires to escape for a few hours, a day, or longer. But I have also led retreats of silence and solitude, using these cabins as housing and retreat for a weekend.

"Come and meet God," has been the invitation.

21.
The Blessings of Solitude
COME WALK WITH ME

I PULLED MY JACKET CLOSER to my body and eased the back screen door closed, not wanting to arouse Vince and Tiger. I considered them my loyal "guard cats," watching for any additional forlorn feral felines that would like to call our farmhouse home. Truth be known, I would welcome more cats into my life. But God seems to have given me a built-in safety mechanism, not only in my guard cats, but also in the garb of Dear Husband who keeps me from over-doing my welcome-every-animal-to-the-farm penchant. Vince and Tiger stretched and came out from under the porch to greet me, but they would have to wait for their handful of dry cat food, because I was on a mission.

Reaching the driveway I crunched my way through snow and ice, past the little workshop, a converted chicken coop. Buck, our yellow lab, was bouncing up and down at the end of his chain, excited at the possibility of being loosed from his own particular guard post—the looming door of the old red barn. Buck's duties included scaring away any unwanted rodent (although he had been known to spend the winter with a family of skunks that had sneaked in the back door of the barn to take refuge in a stack of milled lumber). Buck's other duty, taken on of his own accord, was scaring the daylights out of Vince and Tiger. To Buck, cats were prey—never mind the squirrels and rabbits that inhabited the yard.

Buck loved our early-morning walks. Buck considered my prayer walks pure adventure and delight. He sat obediently as I ran my fingers around his collar, feeling for the metal snap. The instant the snap was loosened, Buck was bouncing again, this time in a circle around me as together we headed past the barn toward the stony road to the pasture above. Finally calmed down, he began to follow rabbit trails, his nose lightly touching the pebbles and tufts of grass, watching my movements out of the corner of his eye.

We made our way beyond the old barn and reached the gate to the pasture. This gate was a gift built by our artistic son, Daniel. He carved into it words that aptly describe my intent for these early morning strolls: "I will lift up my eyes unto the hills from whence cometh my help; my help comes from the Lord."

"Yes, Lord, I am lifting up not only my eyes, but my soul to you this morning," I whispered.

The old glass knob—now aged to an antique lavender—glistened as morning light reflected from the dew settled into its crevices. Unlatching the hook that fit over the knob, I pulled the gate open and walked through onto the tree-lined path.

Ever upward we climbed on this surprisingly non-flat Kansas pathway. The gravel road leads past the outhouse and up a steep incline, through the cedar and oak woods to a high, bluestem pasture, part of what is called the "last stand of the tall grass prairie." These grasslands run from Texas to Canada in a narrow strip where the land has remained unbroken. Less than five percent of the original prairie remains today. Farmer Judd always takes great delight in giving tours of this unique pasture land of grasses: the tall bluestem, the buffalo grass, the side oats, the Indian grass. This is part of God's great eco-system, and our family has become partner in caretaking this small plot of ground. My soul drank in the beauty of this out-of-the-way world.

I commenced my private time of walking and conversing with the God of all time and eternity. Strolling along the beginning of the prayer trail, I practiced shedding all my pretenses. He knows me, and he loves me just as I am. I don't have to pretend that I am worthy of his attention. I don't have to apologize for my not-so-perfect face, my stringy hair, and my rather stumpy legs. For goodness sakes, he is the one who fashioned all of my parts. And he is satisfied. He and I can both agree that I have lots to learn and gobs of maturing to do, but he has promised to not give up on me. For the initial part of my walk, I simply bathe in that love and acceptance.

I do most of the listening up here in this sky-drenched pasture. A comforting solitude is one of the greatest gifts the farm has provided—not just the chance to be alone, but the opportunity to place my body, soul, and spirit into the presence of God without distractions of noise, frenetic activity, and without the need to meet anyone else's expectations. I can simply let God's presence become a blanket of comfort and acceptance around me.

And so in those first steps on the prayer trail I allowed the vestiges of any mask to be gently erased by God's love.

A little uneven with a stubble of grass here and there, this trail has been tractor mowed specifically for anyone who would like to be alone with God. It has been trodden not only by my feet, but by my children, my grandchildren, by neighbors, by friends, by students, by local pastors. It has become hallowed ground. We have all met with God, discussed with God, been encouraged by his presence, and dropped to our knees on this hallowed ground. This particular day, I think of our friend, John Bascom, who wrote his doctoral thesis on the geography of God's presence. It is his strong belief that here, where so many prayers have been laid before God, so many conversations have been carried on in the supernatural realm, that God's presence inhabits this land more palpably than in places inhabited by god-less living. I believe he is right, although I have no evidence or thesis to present on the subject. Perhaps that is for another day's consideration.

As I continued walking, I reached the north fence line where the trail bends and turns west. Buck was still keeping his eye on me while he checked out the buffalo wallow, look-ing for a few laps of water that may still linger in the hole from Tuesday's rain. My thoughts turned to questions I needed to place before God. This particular day, I felt troubled.

A friend I love dearly had been wounded—and those wounds had come from me. Yet, I could not betray what I truly believed was a biblical position. We sat on the same committee, but our hearts were full of pain and, at times, anger. "God, how do I handle this? What do I do with these feelings?" I held up my anguish to him. I was gently reminded of a quote I had written in my prayer journal a few days before, "We just have to walk in the kingdom with others, instead of trying to drive them to change their ways and attitudes" (Willard, *Divine Conspiracy* p. 231). My prayer became, "Please give me wisdom in our encounters to be able to communicate your love."

Gently the Lord's assurance comes, that he is aware of the issue, that he is teaching me through it, and that good would eventually come from it. Did I *feel* this assurance? Nope. But I *knew* it.

I smiled as I rounded the southwest corner fenceline and turned my feet and face toward the east. How many times had I wrestled with my feelings up here on this trail? How many times had God listened to my tears, anger, and questions? Honestly, I think the laments often outweighed the praises. Yet how patient he has been with me!

So I spent the last few minutes focused on the goodness of my Companion.

Turning my face toward the trail that leads down to the farmhouse, I looked for Buck. He had found his buffalo wallow and obviously enjoyed lying in the cool mud; his belly and legs were a chocolate-brown contrast to his yellow back.

"Thank you, God," I whispered. A little more hope, a little more peace had come, reminding me that the *God Who is There* really is there—and here and in me and above me and around me and inside me.

I have loved sharing this walking-with-God path. "Go, listen to God up on the trail," I have said to dear friends and students, fully expecting them to have the same conversations I have had. But not everyone has been able to "hear" God in this way on this path. Hard as it has been for me to understand this "deafness," I have come to accept it.

One of my dearest students had been searching for answers, for a sense of God's presence. I confidently sent her out to walk and listen. She was gone for an hour or more. When she returned, we met in the farmhouse. Sitting beside me on the futon in the front room, she burst into tears.

"Nancy, I didn't hear God at all," she sobbed. "He wasn't there for me. All I saw were trees and grass, and while I was praying I stumbled into a hole, and my Bible and I went sprawling. I am such a klutz; and God is not there, at least not for me."

The words came out in a stream of frustration. I was dumbstruck! I had no answer. She tried so hard yet failed.

Later, this gal and I had a conversation about her experience. "I have decided that I just don't hear God the same way you do, Nancy," she explained. She became a wife and mother, and grew into a wise and godly woman.

I can accept that God speaks to us in our individual heart languages. After all, he wrote all of the languages and placed them in our hearts. This pasture has become one of the strongest expressions of my heart language.

22.
Transformations

AFTER A HEARTY KANSAS POTLUCK, we gathered in the living room, each finding a place to sit. Relaxed but attentive, the students were ready for discussion. Judd opened the meeting by explaining to the students how we planned our yearly conferences, and how we desired to serve them. We were willing to raise the money and do what we could to offer them a conference that would inspire them and meet their needs. "So," Judd concluded by saying, "if we could bring someone to speak, someone you would want to hear, who would that be? Think big. It could be a speaker or a musician. Who would you choose?"

We had called this meeting because we were facing a paradigm shift that we had not seen coming. It was the mid 1990s. The guest for our most-recent Spiritual Dynamics Conference had been a well-known author and sought-after speaker. We made great effort to accommodate more people. We used facilities closer to the campus so more students could come. Then, although young people had always been part of our ministry, few of them attended this time.

We wrestled with questions. Where were the hearts of the young people today? How could we encourage them? Discussion of deep spiritual and theological issues was not drawing them. Or, perhaps we were not bringing in speakers *they* desired to hear or introducing topics they wanted to discuss.

We needed to hear from the young people themselves. So, early the next fall semester we invited about ten students, men and women, to our bi-monthly informal potluck and discussion. These students did not know each other, nor did they know what questions we would ask.

Their responses startled us.

The room was silent for a moment after Judd's probing question. Finally, one student spoke: "I can't think of anyone I want to hear." Another joined in: "No, I don't feel a need to be told anything by someone I don't know personally." Another student added, "We know what to do. We have been told what is right, how to live, how to think. We just want to see what it looks like. I would rather know how that man or woman lives out what he or she believes. What she does in the morning when she gets up, how he loves his wife, how they operate when things don't go well."

These students were hungry for relationships that modeled the Christian life, day in and day out. *Relationship*.

As they left that evening, we were silent. In fact, we were overwhelmed. Creating conferences is difficult enough. But how in the world were we to offer day-to-day relationships, or make ourselves personally available to young people who longed for personal interaction and modeling? What was God doing? Where was he leading us? How would we use our gifts, the farm, and our resources to follow where the current trend was heading?

This phenomena was not something we alone faced. I found the same dilemma when I visited the English L'Abri in

Greatham, England. Young people are looking for family, for a place to belong, and for models. Philosophical and religious discussions are not foremost on their minds. They are looking for community.

Slowly over the next few months we assessed what we had. We had people. We had space. We had resources.

We always recognized the importance of working, growing, learning, serving and sharing together in the body of Christ. Never quite sure what this should look like for us, we probed for examples. No, we decided. We did not want a commune, nor did we feel comfortable about releasing all personal property. Although there are communities who are comfortable with meshing personal identities, we value living diverse lifestyles. We definitely have wrestled with how we should look, how we should define ourselves; but slowly, over these years, we have settled into what works for us, and we have grown into a true community.

When we moved to the farm, we began with a base of friends and college students. Even though we, the Swiharts, owned the land, we *all*—including the college students—considered it *our* land. This land is something God provided for us to use as ministry together. We pooled our gifts: love of adventure, creativity, youthful energy, wisdom, and music. Each person brought his/her own history, gifts, and degree of commitment. We inspired, encouraged, and sometimes corrected each other, all for a common purpose of living out the kingdom in the culture where God has placed us. The outcome is a unique ministry. Together we cleared the land, tore down buildings, built a prayer chapel, built several rustic cabins (all out of recycled materials or harvested trees), and planned conferences.

During the years of settling, becoming, and doing ministry

and conferences, we also became a settled community here on the hundred and sixty acres. Kay Bascom esplained it thus:

> *For those who have not been to the Swihart Farm, it is unusual to describe. Most farms are squarish. This farm is on a quarter mile wide strip that spans a mile long with a "belt" in the middle—a fairly straight Kitten Creek Road which roughly follows a very crooked Kitten Creek. When the Swiharts bought the old Fritz farm in 1982, there were just a scattering of dilapidated buildings west of the road: a house, barns, and sheds.*

Transformed now, I picture the geography in terms of a butterfly with spread wings. Her black body is Kitten Creek Road. Her feelers point southward toward Keats village. Her upper right wing is polka-dotted—no, polka-squared—by the original home, barn, out buildings, plus a shop and the Bethlehem Revisited "set." The Troyers (Sara and her husband, Dan, and their two sons) now live there today. The upper left wing is marked by Dan Swihart's family farm, and Judd and Nancy's new home. The lower right wing now hosts two Bascom homes, and the lower left wing, the Reppert farm.

Many have come to this spot in their chrysalis years, and have flown away into their butterfly pilgrimages. It was here that many of us found reality in Jesus, in fellowship, in creative undertakings together, and in solitude.

We've glimpsed a rich variety of transformations—transformations of land and relationships and experiences.

Since the purchase in 1982, one family home has grown to six. The process seemed to be God-timed. Jay and Sue Reppert, with baby Leta, three-year-old Sarah, and five-year-old Ketty came in the spring of 1985 after a stint in Nigeria to buy and settle on twenty acres of the farm. Jay, a medical doctor, became acquainted with Charles Bascom through the medical facility at Kansas State University. That summer, Charles Bascom and Kay—part of Wellspring from the beginning—bought five acres and built a log home across the road from the Repperts.

Both families, although intricately involved in our community, brought their own unique lifestyles, personalities, and families. The Reppert family settled in to farming their twenty acres (which later grew into fifty acres). Sue homeschooled the children, canned, baked, and worked in their huge garden and orchard. Jay, a physician, is never happier than when he is out in the fields or garden and working with the animals. Although their three daughters and two sons have excelled in the academic world, the Reppert's greatest satisfaction has come in seeing their five children love God and serve him. Their specific ministry brought creativity to our conferences, hospitality for many guests—both internationals and Americans, a great work ethic, and vast knowledge of organic farming.

The Bascoms and their three sons' families have left an indelible mark across the history of our community. Charles, with his background in medical missions in Ethiopia, his pastoral heart, laid-back demeanor, and love for internationals held an important role in life here on the farm. He always had time to talk, listen, and offer guidance that reflected wise biblical principles. Kay—gentle, intelligent, and encouraging—is a warm hostess to the myriad of guests who still find their way to the Bascom home. She is a prolific writer, a sought-after teacher and mentor here in the surrounding community.

About the year 2000, when Nat (the third son of Charles and Kay) and Marcia Bascom and their three children came home from Africa for a year-long furlough, they desired a home in the United States, where they could come on their breaks from Africa. They bought three acres and built a home they designed themselves, across a little meadow from Charles and Kay. After renting out the home while they served in Kenya for years, Nat and Marcia and their three children eventually moved back to the States. By now, Nat, Marcia, and their daughter, Claire, have made their home and family an integral part of the life of the farm.

Two more families live on the farm today. Dan, our second son, along with his wife, NancyLisa, and their nine children, bought almost forty acres, and designed and built their large home down a lane and across Kitten Creek. They have established their little farm with a huge vegetable garden and a myriad of animals and fowls. NancyLisa homeschools the children while Dan works at the local hospital as a physical therapist. Dan co-pastors a small intergenerational church and is the director of what today is our largest outreach, Bethlehem Revisited.

The last family to join us here at the farm, but who were integrally invested even before they moved here, is our daughter Sara (Swihart) Troyer and her husband, Dan. Along with their two sons, they have taken over the old farm house and buildings and oversee what happens there.

Our son-in-law, Dan, is a construction engineer, so part of the plan when they bought our home was to build another one for us. Judd designed the home that is now planted across the road from the farmstead, and Dan Troyer became the foreman of the project. Dan T. and his very small sons, along with our son Dan, the two oldest grandsons, E.J. (15) and Josiah (11), and Judd, worked every evening and Saturdays for a year to erect and finish our wonderful retirement home. Dan's other important job is to orchestrate all the technical and behind-the-scenes work for Bethlehem Revisited.

These families constitute our community on the 160-acre farm. But many other Wellspringers live in the area and, being a college and fort community, many also have come and gone. They, too, fill a huge part in our identity. Continuing our old custom of conferences, we have adapted them to reunions. People come back to the farm from all over the country to celebrate our ongoing history with each other and our deep spiritual bonds.

We have grown in a Spirit-directed way, quite differently from what we envisioned in those early years. Had we forced our early plans and dreams, we would have missed the better plan that God designed. Being redirected—or perhaps re-focused—by the college students who desired relationship, helped us to see ways God was working and how to work along with him.

Being a community ourselves, living out our daily lives as examples of God-followers, not allowing the culture to dictate the direction of our lives, filling our souls with truth, living in relationship with him and with each other, we are living out our kind of community. The rest of ministry would naturally follow. Celebrating together, working together, sharing possessions, worshiping together, and sometimes mourning together: this is our current community. Who knows what else God has planned!

23.
A Purposefully-Chosen Life

THE EVENING WAS COOL AND CLEAR. With our walking sticks in hand, Sarah A., Elizabeth, and I had walked the path past the chapel and down the small ravine to the Bascom home by way of the pasture rather than take the gravel road. Kay warmly welcomed us and we were ushered into their log home to a warm and inspiring visit with Charles and Kay. Later, with our hearts full of a sense of "all is right with the world," we left the cabin and made our way down the stone steps to the driveway and on out to Kitten Creek Road.

Slowing the pace a bit, Elizabeth turned to me and remarked wistfully, "You know, don't you, that you live an enchanted life."

I would ponder that statement throughout the summer. Sarah and Elizabeth were living with us that summer. Earlier, near the end of the spring semester, we had been eating lunch together in the college cafeteria when the subject of housing came up. As students at Manhattan Christian College, they both had jobs in Manhattan for the summer but had not found an affordable place to live. Rent can be quite exorbitant in a college town.

With some hesitation I offered them a place to stay for

the summer, knowing what I had to offer was modest, to say the least. Having visited the farm before, Sarah knew what to expect; but I explained to Elizabeth.

"Our house is quite small [by this time we had added a bedroom and bathroom to the nine-hundred-fifty square-foot home], but we do have a bedroom and bath in the cellar that the boys aren't using any more. It's rustic. But we could let you share that space for no rent, if you help a little with meal preparations." A deal they could not refuse!

That was 1993, a historic summer in Manhattan. Beginning with promise, it ended with tornadoes and floods. Flooded out of the basement, the girls ended up sharing a small bedroom near the living room. But it worked. And they gave me a perspective on our lifestyle that was both humbling and encouraging.

"An enchanted life," Elizabeth called it. Yes, we were blessed! It didn't just happen, though. Ours has been an intentional life. We are a mixture of young people and old people; introverts and extraverts; we don't all go to the same church; some of us love to garden and farm, and some of us don't; some home school, some don't; from physician, to physical therapist, to engineer, to college professor, to marriage counselor, our "day jobs" have brought different expertise and interests. So what draws us into a lifestyle of community? How does it look with such a variety of interests and people?

Living in community means living with a commitment to one another and a commitment to the One who indwells us. We love each other, and we love our Creator.

Together over the years we lived out the seasons of Ecclesiastes 3. We celebrated the births of babies, each child a precious gift from God. The children grew within the boundaries of love and encouragement to be all they were created to be, and to follow their bent.

Together we celebrated Jewish feasts and meals. With Kay and Charles's love for Israel and the Jewish people, and their study of the Messiah in both the Old and New Testament, we gained a better understanding of God's calendar, his prophetic seasons, and we developed a love for God's people, the Jews. The rhythm of Jewish celebrations is God's way of preparing his people for the coming Messiah, both first and second comings.

We began in the middle of the 1980s by celebrating a Seder. As a community we prepared the Seder and invited the larger church community in Manhattan. With a Messianic Jewish couple leading the service, we experienced a renewed appreciation for the unique way God communicates deep truths through symbolic and meaningful activities. For several years we continued to offer community Seders until others caught the vision and began doing their own. Today, families are encouraged to celebrate in their own homes; and occasionally we get together in our own community to walk through the now-familiar traditional Seder meal.

One of the celebrations children especially enjoy is preparing and celebrating the Feast of Booths which comes in the fall. Along with the dads, the children help build a booth or tabernacle. The sukkots or booths are a reminder of the temporary homes that the Israelites lived in while they wandered in the desert forty years. It also reminds us that we are pilgrims looking forward to reaching our permanent home in eternity. We decorate the booths with flowers, vegetables, and fruit as a reminder of the harvest. In the evening, families gather and we walk through the "wave offering," circling the booth and singing a song of blessing and thanksgiving.

At one point in the Jewish ceremony, the priest would pour water over the altar. In our celebration we have a child slowly pour water from a pitcher, during which we read from scripture the words Jesus spoke as he celebrated the Feast: "If anyone thirsts, let him come to Me and drink. He who believes in Me, as the Scripture has said, out of his heart will flow rivers of living water" (John 7:37-38).

The Bascoms inspired us in these endeavors, bringing richness to the community. Charles, with his adaption of a shofar, led us down to the creek to celebrate the *tashlich*, a ritual many Jews observe during Rosh HaShanah. "Tashlich" means "casting off" in Hebrew and involves symbolically casting off the sins of the previous year by tossing pieces of bread or another food into a body of flowing water.

Is there any better way to demonstrate to children what repentance and forgiveness means? God knows the importance of symbolism, of physically taking part in an act that enters not only the mental and rational part of our being, but cements it into our souls through experience.

When God gave us that run-down farm, he had hidden treasures planted for us to discover and use. Every little part of this gift could be used in various ways of celebration. To stand back and see the possibilities of celebration takes a little vision. We had hills, valleys, woods, and a creek. We also had a hand-dug root cellar in our side yard partially facing the road. The cellar had a beautiful arched-roof with hand-stacked limestone. I am sure the original owners, the Fritz's, stored their canned goods there. How would *we* use it? … For the empty tomb, of course!

With a tall hill overlooking the valley and an empty tomb, what naturally follows is a celebration of Resurrection Sunday. Sometimes a few, sometimes a crowd will meet at the tomb long before sunrise on that special morning. The tomb is adorned with flowers at the entrance. Inside, just visible in the flickering candlelight, sits a bench where grave cloths lie empty and folded. Together, we silently wind our way up the trail to the top of the pasture where benches are arranged round an empty cross. There, one person leads a short devotion. Then, as the sun rises over the hill across the road, we burst into song.

Breakfast together in the barn completes the celebration.

In the 1980s, one September we stumbled onto another community celebration. The Bascom family stepped in to fill a temporary leadership role in a program our church started called Helping International Students (or HIS). Since the university did not hold classes on Labor Day, the Bascoms thought it a good idea to offer a barbecue picnic at the farm for any international who would like to come.

Thinking maybe twenty to thirty students would take up the invitation, we began grilling chicken at a large grill out by the barn. American friends contributed potato salad, chips, and fruit. At the appropriate time, the first carload of international students arrived. And then another and another.

I still remember Kay's eyes as she came into the kitchen where I was scrambling to find more food. "Nancy, they just keep coming!" Both excitement and anxiety filled her eyes.

Fortunately, months earlier, Judd and I had purchased a large quantity of quick-frozen chicken legs and thighs. I scurried down to the basement and started pulling chicken out of the freezer, and handing it to Kay. Soon we had a little relay race going from the freezer to the grill.

By the end of the evening, we had fed a hundred-and-twenty internationals, and on the stone wall where we had served the meals, one full plate of food remained, a surplus that assured us

God is still in the business of feeding the multitudes. This celebration of the international Labor Day picnic we continued at the farm for several years until the attendance reached over three hundred and fifty, forcing us to move to a larger venue.

Celebrations! Neighborhood potlucks, picnics, weddings, reading the Declaration of Independence on the Fourth of July, baptisms in Kitten Creek, sunrise services on Resurrection Sunday, and a living nativity at Christmas. These celebrations seem to hallow the land on which they take place.

However, not all of life is filled with gaiety and happy celebrations. Our community is also planted in the fallen world, and like everyone else, we face the inevitable results. Therefore, we also mourn together. The death of Charles Bascom weighed heavily on our community because of his larger-than-life presence—not only on Kitten Creek Road, but across the globe. I wrote this piece the day he died:

In writing a book my thoughts have been focused on what was. How did God create a place of worship and community out of an old ramshackle farm? I have marveled at his presence, his gifts, and his transformations.

Today I am forced to take a deeper look at what is, and perhaps a little of what is to come. The present lies heavy upon us, but God is present. The future is behind a curtain, but God is there, also.

This past week we lost the "pastor" of our community, Charles Bascom. The loss of Charles's presence will be felt deeply by us all. But there is also celebration in the fact that he is no longer weighted down with infirmities, the result of our fallen world.

His life blessed us in ways that formed much of who we have become. He was the wise patriarch who continually pointed us to Scripture, prayer, and celebration. His life was a gift, given in time but now continuing in eternity. We will celebrate that gift at his memorial service. And in the future we will continue to celebrate through our lives that have been enriched and changed because of Charles.

We have lost others here at the farm: a grandmother, a still-born granddaughter, a grandfather, a teenaged son. Yet the loss is only temporary. We will see them again when we step into the "what is to come" of Heaven. We celebrate the promise of that gift.

People are gifts. Each person who has entered our lives has brought the gift of who they are. Those gifts have come from the Giver, and through the years we have received those gifts and been changed through those gifts. We have unwrapped them and celebrated God's presence in them.

The deep sorrow of these losses has been eased because of the presence of those who not only love us, but knew and loved the one we lost. We can encourage each other through the steps of grieving, and sometimes simply the presence of others is a reminder of the God who is always there (as Francis Schaeffer would put it).

Together we "walk through the shadow of death." And our Shepherd is with us.

SECTION FOUR

The Gift of a Story

24.
An Idea Is Born

BY OUR SECOND YEAR ON THE FARM, we had acquired two horses and a few sheep. Many dark evenings I would walk to the barn, fill the grain buckets, toss some hay, break the ice in the water tanks, then stand and enjoy the scene playing out before me. After the first general excitement of feeding time, the animals would settle down to contentedly nibble their hay.

In the quiet, I leaned against the barnyard gate and reminisced, reflecting on the unique celebrations we had experienced back in California. Polished church programs drew thousands. We would dress in our best and with great anticipation enter the auditorium. We were handed a program and ushered to our seats; then we waited in excitement, along with a crowd of two-thousand spectators, for this one-of-a-kind performance. At last the house lights dimmed, and the curtain rose. We were enthralled with the talent and with the props. The message was nostalgic, and we were "Christmased."

Under the brilliant stars of the Kansas sky, I looked around at a pastoral scene. Snow padded the rocks and ground with white softness. The unpretentious atmosphere provided a quiet reminder of the first Christmas. No red carpet, just trails of manure, hay, and dirt. No dignitaries, just the residents of the stable. No gold-lined crib, just a hand-hewn wooden manger where the sheep and donkeys eat. In the presence of these simple creatures, God's Son was born. Watching my horses and sheep chomp their hay, I imagined the creatures in the stable of old went on about their business of eating and resting. They continued in their simple "isness" of just being sheep, being goats, being horses (or perhaps camels).

As I drank in the wonder of that December evening, I thought of the reality I was so privileged to witness. No pretense, no glare of spotlight, no loud parties or raucous laughter. Reality, simplicity: this was the scene into which the God of the universe had chosen to send his Son: a real woman and a real man; and a real stable full of real animal smells and unimpressed animal life. No one was there to clean up the place, to set up the lights, to sterilize the manger.

And so began a dream to share this simple experience with others, to bathe their imaginations with the wonder of entering into the world of the infant Savior. By the following Christmas, this idea became a reality.

It was a late December evening, and the sun had set on Kitten Creek Road. The little community of Wellspring was ready to experience our very own nativity celebration. Judd and I led the animals down the gravel road, Judd holding the lead ropes to the horse and pony, and I with my bucket of grain for the sheep. Darkness enveloped us except for the beam from the flashlight Judd held in his right hand. At the bottom of the hill, we turned in to the pole shed area, the designated spot for our first nativity program.

We chose the pole shed area because of the nice round bales stored in the shed; and the meadow, covered with rich brome, was familiar territory to the animals.

The germ of an idea grew into a plan, and that plan was being carried out by all of our Wellspring group. The beauty of community! The preparation was basic. One of the mothers found a pattern for angel wings and made some simple white costumes. We had a Mary and Joseph in bathrobes and shawls, a baby wrapped in a beautiful white blanket, and a narrator dressed in white. The script was scripture from Luke, and the songs were carols we all knew.

We tied the horses near the hay and put the sheep near the manger. Someone hung a couple of lanterns and built a fire in the fire pit. We gathered round the fire and waited for others to arrive. Slowly the moms and dads, children and college students began to join us around the fire. We were ready. The two- and three-year-old children were lifted up on the large bales where they perched, reminding us of angels that surely watched at the manger.

When everyone gathered, we passed out a simple white sheet with the Scripture verses we would read interspersed with a few carols. The program started with Luke chapter 2. The first reader began:

> In those days Caesar Augustus issued a decree that a census should be taken of the entire Roman world. (This was the first census that took place while Quirinius was governor of Syria.) And everyone went to their own town to register.

The second reader continued:

> So Joseph also went up from the town of Nazareth in Galilee to Judea, to Bethlehem the town of David, because he belonged to the house and line of David. He went there to register with Mary, who was pledged to be married to him and was expecting a child. While they were there, the time came for the baby to be born, and

she gave birth to her firstborn, a son. She wrapped him in cloths and placed him in a manger because there was no guest room available for them.

Now we focused on the manger. Ah, the simple, the quiet, the holy. And we sang quietly, "Silent night, holy night." Yes, all was calm, all was bright. We continued through the rest of the story, the sheep and little shepherds adding ambiance to the experience.

At one point we were interrupted by one of the little angels protesting loudly, "Mommy, the horse is eating my hay bale! Make him stop!" We all giggled, someone repositioned the horse, and the next reader continued the story:

And there were shepherds living out in the fields nearby, keeping watch over their flocks at night. An angel of the Lord appeared to them, and the glory of the Lord shone around them, and they were terrified. But the angel said to them, "Do not be afraid. I bring you good news that will cause great joy for all the people. Today in the town of David a Savior has been born to you; he is the Messiah, the Lord. This will be a sign to you: You will find a baby wrapped in cloths and lying in a manger.

Suddenly a great company of the heavenly host appeared with the angel, praising God and saying,

Glory to God in the highest heaven, and on earth peace to those on whom his favor rests.

At this point, the angels had a chance to sing their hearts out. "Angels we have heard on high …" One little angel in particular stuck out her chest, filled her lungs, and sang at the top of her pint-sized voice, "Gloooooooooriah, in egg shells see glory." With amusement I wondered what God might have in store for this little angel. Today that little angel, Leta, has become a grown-up angelic singer and server in the kingdom of God.

We finished the evening with the rest of the passage:

The shepherds returned, glorifying and praising God for all the things they had heard and seen, which were just as they had been told.

At the end of the service, after putting out the fire in the pit, and gathering up the horse and sheep, we headed from the meadow to the road and back to the house for hot chocolate.

This was an experience we would replay in our memories for a long time.

25.
The Vision Grows
~The Second Phase~

WE DID CONTINUE TO CELEBRATE our version of a nativity pageant, eventually inviting others to join us. Progressing from the single scene in the pole shed area, we had moved the pageant to the area around the barn and hillside. We had grown from a single-scene nativity to a re-enactment with several scenes that required people to move from one place to another.

By the early 1990s our participants had grown, also. The nativity had attracted a small group of dedicated folks who were helping to plan the event. I drafted some students from the drama club at the college; from church we were blessed with a couple of talented and dedicated acting enthusiasts. To spread the word, we began to advertise on the local radio station.

We were offering something that started as a vision God imprinted on my heart, but others quickly adopted the idea. It was evident: God had given us this land of hills, trees, valleys, and open fields with an "empty tomb" in the guise of a stone cellar built into the hill. The story was written into its very geography.

I am a dreamer, not a director; but until others came along to carry the mantle of directing, the job fell to me.

One year, the majority of our cast were college students, who are always fresh, enthusiastic, creative, and energetic. To that list of descriptors that year, though, we had to add the word "stressed" because we managed to schedule the event the weekend before finals. That was *one* of our mistakes.

The other mistake was having no rehearsal. On the day of the event, just an hour or so before people were to arrive, a touch of bedlam prevailed. It began when the guys with the microphone for Mary (who was to give a beautiful soliloquy from Max Lucado's *Jesus Came Near*) arrived late, without the proper equipment.

As I worked to solve problems with the tech guys, I was standing near the sheep pen. I noticed the "shepherds" having trouble with the sheep that had decided they wouldn't leave the security of the barnyard to follow loud, young men in strange clothing. How to get them up the hill to the place designated as their "set"? A bucket of grain, which had always worked for me when leading the sheep, was of no avail this time. The sheep rebelled, refusing to co-operate.

Leaving the microphone quandary, I helped the would-be shepherds find ropes and coax the sheep in the right direction. I waited at the top of the hill until the sheep were in place around the shepherds' campfire.

Going back to check on the progress of the microphones, I caught sight of a truck stuck in the driveway that led to the pasture. The driver was spinning his wheels while several other students were hand pushing from behind. This truck which would provide the shining lights on the angelic host finally made it up the hill. As it approached the shepherd's campfire, the sheep, already on high alert, became terrified of the strange vehicle and frantically ran back down the hill to the safety of their pen.

However, now that the sheep had ropes, I could leave the shepherding to the shepherds. They would certainly earn their title by the time they got their sheep back up the hill.

From the manger scene, I made my way to the top of our two-story barn where the guests were to be seated later, the prophets were to make their prophecies, and the crowd would be introduced to a desperate Mary and Joseph looking for a place to stay. The benches were organized in rows facing the large roller doors where these several scenes would occur. We were in pretty good shape there, so I was beginning to feel comfortable.

With half an hour left before the guests arrived, I dashed to the house to finish cleaning up from our evening meal. A few cups and dirty dishes sat on the counter, so I ran some water in the sink and grabbed a cup to immerse in the hot soapy water. "Hurry" is not my strong suit; in fact, I have a tendency to be clumsy as my mind becomes disengaged from my fingers. As I started to dunk the last cup into the water, it fell from my fingers. Without thinking, I grabbed the cup as it shattered in the sink. Pulling my hands from the soapy water, I looked at the blood beginning to spurt from the middle finger on my right hand. Not good!

Trying to stop the bleeding, we realized it was going to require some "doctor" attention. A trip to the ER was out of the question at this point. Judd, having returned to the house from his work with the preparations, decided we should call our "doctor in residence" Charlie Bascom.

It only took a few minutes for Charles to arrive. Looking closely at my finger, he agreed. "Yes, this should have some stitches, but ... perhaps we could put a butterfly Band-Aid on it and find something to stabilize it." Looking around the kitchen, he queried, "Do you have a spoon?"

Of course, we did. But we thought he might be joking.

However, after cleaning the cut and applying a Band-Aid, Charles took a spoon from the kitchen drawer, laid it along my finger, and began wrapping the spoon and finger together tightly. Now I sported the bowl of the spoon protruding from the top of my bandaged finger. There was no time to commiserate or to ponder how to adapt to this new appendage. The show must go on.

Quickly I pulled on woolen gloves to hide the strange specter, donned my army jacket and rushed out to the barn where the guests were already assembling. The barn was filled with people—more people than we had anticipated—bundled in coats and hats, milling around.

I stepped into the barn and my neighbor Sharon rushed up to me. She had a kindly-looking gentleman in tow, who she excitedly introduced. "Nancy, I would like you to meet my priest, Father R. I have been telling him about this and am so excited for him to meet you."

"Welcome, Father." I smiled and extended my right hand to shake his. As quickly as I had offered it, I pulled my hand back and blurted, "Oh, I'm so sorry! I can't shake your hand; I have a spoon on my finger."

No sooner did those words leave my lips than another guest came up to talk. The crowd closed between the priest and me and I never saw him again that evening. That poor man was left to his own conclusions about the "spoon on my finger."

The program was about to begin. As the audience took their seats, the lights were dimmed, and the first prophet made his appearance.

"Ah, Lord God," I breathed, "please bring your presence and peace to this place and to the guests."

In spite of the chaos going on about us, at the core of it all was God offering his message of transcendent truth. At that first appearance of the baby Savior, he had interrupted a busy scene with no room left in the inns, a gathering that was probably not any more peaceful than the one I was experiencing. In all the chaos of crowds and noise and smells, and in the pain and messiness of birth, the Prince of Peace had entered our fallen world.

The audience quieted as a knock came on the large, rolling barn door. The Innkeeper strode to the door and rolled it open. There in the darkness stood Joseph, motioning toward a pregnant Mary sitting on a donkey close behind him. With urgency he explained their plight: "Please, sir, can you give us a room for the night? My wife is about to deliver, and we have nowhere to stay."

"Can't you see," shouted Jim, our surly innkeeper as he turned and waved with a sweeping arm across the audience, "we are full tonight."

Ah, we were finally on track. An experience of remembrance and worship was beginning to take place.

As Mary and Joseph left to find the stable, the audience was invited to join in singing, "O Come O Come, Emmanuel" in the dimly-lit barn.

It was time for the crowd to move to the next scene.

As together we trudged up the hillside, the beautiful voice of an "angel" caroled us singing, "I Wonder As I Wander." The words to the song echoed through the calm, winter air:

> *I wonder as I wander out under the sky,*
> *Why Jesus the Savior did come for to die.*
> *For poor lonely people like you and like I*
> *I wonder as I wander, out under the sky.*

We joined the shepherds on the hill around the crackling

bonfire. The sheep were held tightly in hand. Suddenly, Gabriel came forward out of the darkness.

"Behold!"

Shepherds fell to the earth in fear.

Gabriel gave his startling announcement, then truck lights came on and beamed upon the angels standing on the hillside. "Glory to God in the highest," they declared and began singing the first part of the Hallelujah chorus.

We all, along with the shepherds, felt wonder and amazement.

The truck lights went out, the angels disappeared into the darkness, and the crowd was invited to follow the shepherds to find this promised baby "wrapped in swaddling clothes and lying in a manger."

We began our trek across the field, coming to the spot where, from the pasture, we could look down on the tiny village of Keats. As we stopped to watch the village lights twinkling in the blackness of the night, our hearts and thoughts filled with reverence.

"Oh little town of Bethlehem, how still we see thee lie," we sang softly and reverently, imagining we were there in that holy land the very night the tiny King was born. Then we followed the shepherds and their sheep on the trek toward Bethlehem.

This procedure should have worked, except in the dark the shepherds—our would-be leaders—got lost, and the crowd began wandering like the Israelites in the desert. My sheep were not accustomed to a crowd of people following them around in the darkness, nor did they know the voices of these strangers.

Finally, not liking the disorientation, the sheep escaped and high-tailed it down a ravine to the safety of their pen. One lone sheep remained in the pasture on a lead rope. On the other end of the tether was a very determined and somewhat successful shepherd.

The lone sheep, Charlie, my gentle giant as I fondly called him, was none too happy about losing the rest of the flock. When I finally got to the front of the crowd, the shepherd leading Charlie whispered in frustration, "Mrs. Swihart, I can't get this sheep to do anything." Taking the lead rope from him, I nudged and pulled Charlie in the right direction until he headed down the proper trail. Recognizing me, he became compliant and grudgingly allowed the crowd to follow him and his flock of shepherds down the path to the back side of the barn. The shed was lit by several lanterns illuminating the stone walls. Here lay Baby Jesus in the straw-filled manger, Mary and Joseph standing proudly beside him.

Everything seemed to be in place. Mary and Joseph had found the stable; Mary had birthed the tiny baby. A peaceful, blessed scene. Angels stood in the background and signed in American sign language words to "Away In the Manger," as the audience reverently joined in with their voices. It was all quite beautiful.

Then came Mary's monolog:

> *O infant God. Heaven's fairest child. Conceived by the union of divine grace with our disgrace. Sleep well. Sleep well. Bask in the coolness of this night bright with diamonds. Sleep well, for the heat of anger simmers nearby. Enjoy the silence of the crib, for the noise of confusion rumbles in your future. Savor the sweet safety of my arms, for a day is soon coming when I cannot protect you.*

As you may remember, the tech guys had been working on installing a mic. That mic was now hidden in Mary's shawl. As she began, it became apparent there was no amplification. All the crowd could see was Mary mumbling into her shawl.

An apparent failure. No great thoughts were transmitted to the crowd that night. In retrospect, perhaps the great Director himself over-ruled my fine plans. Scripture itself testifies only that Mary "pondered these things in her heart."

The shepherds were bowing at the manger. The scene finished, they left to spread the good news, and it was time (according to the script) for the three kings to arrive.

Poised in their beautiful costumes, ready to enter the scene with their horses (no camels available) the wisemen were skipped by a misguided narrator. Jumping to the next scene, Mary and Joseph followed the narrator's cue and slowly made their way to the temple where Simeon and Ann were to bless the child.

Oh, but we could not forget the wisemen in their beautiful costumes with their nervous horses. Running around behind the crowd while Simeon was giving his blessing, I tried to quietly, but quickly, get around the crowd to the wisemen. A wooden gate by the water tank was in my way. Gingerly climbing over the old, locked gate, I stepped on a rotting rung, and the whole gate came crashing down along with me. Surely nobody heard, I hoped. Picking myself up, I continued to the confused wisemen. "Go!" I whispered loudly, "Go!!"

As the crowd sang the closing carol, "Joy to the World," the wisemen rushed in and bowed low to the ground for the final chorus. Not the way we had planned it, but it worked, and probably the heavenly Director, himself, was smiling at this revision to my own dramatic and inaccurate interpretation.

Later that evening, after the crowds had left, when all the lighting was extinguished, animals fed and back in their pens, my heart entered into the stillness of the evening. Quietness surrounded me. I gazed at the brilliant stars in the night sky. In the backdrop of God's world, nothing had changed. Peace, beauty, and wonder were here all along, inspite of my chaos.

Work and worship are not exclusive of each other. Working to make it possible for others to worship is sometimes difficult. In my working to achieve the worship opportunity for others, I had not been able to enter fully into that experience myself. Yet peace was portrayed: in the scenes, through the scenes, above the scenes. And, hopefully, that peace was felt and received by the participants.

"Oh, God," I breathed, "let the true meaning of this story continue to reach out and seep into the cracks and crannies of people's hearts, so they might have just a glimpse of the profound message of this Peace Child who came to bring his peace to the earth."

26.
Annual Christmas Pageant
~THE THIRD PHASE~

FAST FORWARD A FEW YEARS. We were entering what I call our third phase.

As our guide, Dr. P., the Old Testament professor at Manhattan Christian College, led our group down the knoll, the lantern he carried provided our only light. We approached a small cabin, the staged home of Mary and Joseph. Through the window, we could discern a couple sitting at the table, apparently enjoying their evening meal by candlelight. But a terrible commotion was coming from behind the cabin.

Immediately the source of the noisy ruckus became evident to us all as out of the darkness a white horse appeared, galloping full speed toward the onlookers. In unison, the group gasped. Just before charging us head-on, the wild steed took a sharp left and disappeared from view. As the horse and rider hurtled past the startled audience, we caught a glimpse of a disheveled Roman soldier hanging on tightly, his helmet dangling precariously from his head.

Without missing a beat, Dr. P. turned to his shocked audience. "Now, that would be the Roman soldier," he explained. "He was supposed to tell Mary and Joseph to go to their home place to register for a census." With great composure, he continued to explain the census and the importance of the decree to the young couple behind the window.

Inside the house we could see Mary and Joseph packing their belongings into a cloth satchel. We watched as they came out of the house, loaded the donkey, and began to walk away into the darkness.

Now Dr. P. led us away from the scene. As we walked up the knoll to the barn, he explained to us, "We are going to an inn this evening and we'll try to find a room for the night. Follow me."

I lagged behind the group, wanting to check on the poor horse and rider. In the darkness I could see them emerge from the barnyard. The soldier was carrying his helmet; his uniform was a bit torn and dirty.

"Are you OK, Ryan?" I whispered, catching up to him. I chose this particular student to be my soldier because he was a skilled rider. He had lots of experience training and breaking horses. But Shiny, my Arab, was a bit unpredictable, even for an experienced rider.

"Yeah," my soldier grumbled. "I was talking to my cousin who had come over by the manger, and I lost track of time. When I saw the group coming, I ran over to the horse. But just as I jumped on her, she bolted. I guess I scared her," he said disgustedly. Cowboys don't like nervous horses much. He motioned to the darkness of the barnyard. "She lost me out there by the water tank. But I caught her again, easy."

Yep, easy-does-it works for Shiny; cowboys are not her style. I helped Ryan straighten his costume, dust off, and secure the helmet on his head. Shiny was still a little agitated and nervous, but Ryan would be more careful now; she had gained his respect.

The rest of my group were at the barn by now, so I decided to go down to the pole shed area to join another group waiting to begin their tour. Parents, children, and college students were warming themselves around a large, brightly-burning bonfire, waiting for the horse-drawn wagon to pick up the next load. The beautiful draft horses and refurbished wagon were a delightful addition to the drama. These horses with their driver would deposit the guests at the foot of the hill by the house where the guests would be met by their guide, Mr. D., another professor from the college. We were trying to space the groups so they would not interfere with the previous group's experience. We were experimenting with how to better accommodate the large crowds who had been coming in recent years.

Every year we were finding more interest and enthusiasm for our Christmas pageant. It had become impossible to take one large group around. People could not hear what was being said, and it took too long to get the large group assembled at each of the six stations.

After much discussion, our volunteer group of visionaries decided we needed to divide the people into smaller groups and have guides lead them through the scenes. It was a big step in logistics that required guides to know scripture and be accustomed to speaking and shepherding people.

Our little college was quite involved in those mid years, and in this new phase we needed an actual script for the guides. Dr. P. pulled together a script for us entitled, *"The Annual Swihart Christmas Pageant: December 15, 1996."*

The first guides of this new phase were three professors and their wives from the college. Our cast was made up of college students, many of whom were given the choice by one of the professors of either writing an eight-page report for their final

Bible assignment, or being in the pageant. We had a good supply of volunteer cast that year! Jim, the surly innkeeper and staunch visionary of our group, called these sometimes-unpredictable cast members "conscripts," which seemed to be a fitting description for them.

You could call us a rag-tag but joyful and expectant mixture of people: the visionaries, the professors, the conscripts, all under the leadership of a mighty God who empowers with his Spirit and brings his message alive through his people.

27.
Bethlehem Revisited
~THE GRAND PHASE~

DECEMBER 3, 2015. Christmas comes early on the farm! Everyone here is knee-deep and prayer-deep in preparing for the thirty-first year of what we now call Bethlehem Revisited. Anticipation fills our hearts as we grandparents along with our children and grandchildren are joined by our large community to worship and work together in bringing this narrative to life once again.

As more and more people attended the pageant, the need for staff and actors has continued to grow. We now need close to one hundred in costume and over a hundred behind the scenes, far more than our small community can provide. Our local Grace Baptist Church helped more and more over the years and finally became the official sponsor of Bethlehem Revisited. People from area churches have taken on roles they love. The guides, prophets, narrators, angels, shepherds, villagers, tech crew and welcome center staffers return year after year to serve in a capacity they see as their personal ministry. Since we don't charge for the tickets, Grace Baptist also financially supports this as an outreach ministry and part of Church life.

No longer do I have the responsibility of directing this

production; in fact, we have had wonderful support from those who were gifted in directing. Today, and for the past ten years, our son, Dan, has taken over the directorship. Following in the path of those before, his godly care over the script and the production has brought a depth of spiritual life that is communicated vibrantly to the thousands of guests who come each year.

Our son-in-law, Dan T., works closely with him as he oversees the technical part of the event. Paths need to be re-laid with wood chips, some paths need to be mowed, the village refurbished, blinds set up for the angels, fire pits rebuilt and stocked with wood, lanterns rounded up and hung. That is a short and inadequate list of all that is required. Dan T. directs the work days and has a small crew who work with him throughout the three evenings.

Before Thanksgiving, costumes are brought from the church where they are stored in tubs. Wooden clothes racks are carried down from storage and set up in the barn. Then our granddaughters lead the assembling of each costume, hanging them in the barn separated into categories: angels, marketplace, shepherds, guides, children, Marys, Josephs, prophets and narrators, to make it easier for each actor and actress to find the right costume before the event each evening. They will all choose their costumes at the dress rehearsal the weekend before Thanksgiving.

The thousands of free, time-staggered tickets that sat in Judd's office have been distributed to various outlets. Stock pens for all the animals that will need boarding overnight are ready and waiting for their occupants. The lanterns (around sixty of them) sit on tables in the barn; some will hang from lampposts, others will hang from the guides' and guide assistants' outstretched arms as they lead the groups through the forty-five minute walk. Orderly stacks of cut wood stand beside the fifteen fire pits.

With prayerful anticipation we have asked God to drench these three nights in his Spirit. We have invited our guests to relive the greatest story we humans can ever tell. In fact, last year, as one woman prepared to board the bus back to the welcome center, she hesitated, then addressed her guide. "You mean to tell me," she almost stammered, "this story is true?"

Without hesitation he answered, "Oh, the amazing thing is, it *is* true!"

Join me now as we experience
a little of Bethlehem Revisited....

Today is Saturday, the last day of the event for this year. We anticipate a lot of activity on the farm all day, as we have had for the past three days. The younger tech guys arrive first, showing up by 10:00 this morning, a little later than usual. Dan, their father and director, let them sleep in since they were busy till after midnight last night—bedding down all the animals, cleaning clutter from the trails, putting out fires, and returning all the thermoses and food bins to the kitchen—so a little extra sleep in the morning to give them the energy for working all the way through evening of our last day.

About 2:30 the kitchen crew arrives at the farmhouse, unloading the frozen soups, cookies, breads and other supplies for this evening's cast and crew. They will be busy in the kitchen fixing sandwiches, making hot chocolate, heating up soups, and filling bins with cakes, veggies, soups and crackers for the cast, which the tech crew will deliver to various stations through the long evening. These snacks have a vital role to play as the cast stands in freezing December weather four to five hours, three nights in a row.

At 4:00 the farm explodes with activity. Cars, trucks, and vans begin to arrive, their occupants spilling out as they head across the road to the farmyard. I love this time of the Bethlehem Revisited days. The farm is transformed from its quiet, mundane existence to a life of vibrant expectancy. Something is about to happen, and only God can breathe life into it.

After the cast members find and don their costumes in the barn, everyone meets at the foot of the tall, rugged cross erected for the tour. The cross's significance brings our attention to the purpose of our message. We meet in total dependence on his grace. The empty tomb, the very next station, reminds us of his victory. As we sing together, "In Christ Alone" we are reminded of the story we are telling … and why we are telling it.

> *In Christ alone, Who took on flesh,*
> *Fullness of God in helpless babe!*
> *This gift of love and righteousness…*

After a short biblical reminder and challenge from Dan, both young and old offer spontaneous prayers. Darkness is falling. It is nearing 5:00, when the first group will arrive. We are finally dismissed to our various locations, and as we disperse, we sense God's blessing. He has begun his work of the evening first in us.

A loud, heavy vehicle is coming down Kitten Creek Road. Without looking we all know it is the first busload of guests for this evening. These guests have already been welcomed at the Keats Park Welcome Center by contagiously hospitable volunteers from Grace Baptist.

For the past few weeks the women have been baking

thousands of cookies. The Welcome Center has its own crew of dedicated servants, from those who welcome each guest, to those who serve the hot chocolate and cookies; from the music ensembles, to the bus group organizers and bus loaders.

The bus riders are now anticipating an adventure as they are transported down the half-mile gravel road and unloaded at Nat Bascom's drive. The lights in the house have been dimmed and, since the house is hidden behind trees, as far as the guests know, they are indeed at the beginning of "the prophet's hill."

Meanwhile, the prayer group has assembled in our darkened home waiting for the cards. One of the tech crew will be delivering the "census" cards. Each guest has filled out a card and will hand it to the Roman census taker at the gate of Bethlehem, as he and his soldiers demand them. For a census has been commanded! These cards are their tickets-become-census-cards and contain their names, etc. The prayer group will spend the evening into the late night lifting up each guest in prayer, by name.

The first trip I always take is before the guests arrive. For a month or more it has been my duty to sit at a recruiting table at church and make sure we filled all of the casting spots. Today I carry the sheet with me, give one to Dan, and we both check each position. Later, I will walk through with a group, mainly to stay connected with what God is doing. On these evenings, the sense of God's presence is palpable.

I have slowed down considerably these days. Now I steal away from the crowds and find a comfortable seat on the porch rocking chair bundled against the cold night air. Three buses are parked on the road, waiting for groups to finish. Another bus-load of guests lumbers down the gravel road.

Over the three nights, some two-thousand people will walk

these Bethlehem paths in groups of fifteen to fifty, led by a guide's lantern as he introduces them to each interactive scene.

In the cold night air I can hear the angels singing up on the hill, while the prophet Micah on the prophet's hillside is proclaiming his message to another group that is slowly working its way toward the village of Bethlehem. This is my personal time of prayer and worship as I recognize God working his miracles in this place and in the hearts of those who have come.

By midnight tonight, the farm will be quiet. The tech crew will have put out all the fires, gathered up the last of the food bins from each station, and bedded down the animals one last time. Then we close the book on one more year of Bethlehem Revisited.

God be praised!

28.
A Dog, a Donkey, and an Old Soul

AS DAKOTA AND I CROSSED THE BROME FIELD and headed toward the farm, I glanced over my shoulder. The sight of an upset donkey caused me to hesitate. Don Quixote (Donk) was stomping, stretching his head above the fence, and working himself up for a loud, obnoxious bray. Dakota, the black lab, and Donk had forged an unusual friendship during Dakota's short stay with her "grandparents." While her family, the Troyers, spent almost a year over in Utah for a job assignment, Dakota became a walking companion and resident at Oma and Opa's home. (You know by now that I am a soft touch when it comes to animals.)

Doubling back, I grabbed Donk's lead rope and opened the gate. Satisfied that he had been understood, he offered me his chin, and I fastened the rope to his halter. This day three of us would walk the trails.

We began our walk on the "hill of the prophets." For years I had gazed out our bedroom window at the cedar forest—untamed but holding much potential. This day the hillside forest sported a wood-chipped path winding up the steep hillside past the Bethlehem Revisited prophet stations: Moses, David, Isaiah, and Micah. (Each prophet has his own fire pit and lantern stand to welcome groups that come past.)

We reached Micah's spot then took a sharp turn to where the guide begins to tell the group that much time has elapsed and the time of Jesus' birth is approaching.

Dakota decided to visit Nat and Marcia's dog, Sheba, since we were so close to her house, hidden in the midst of cedars to the north. I interrupted my climb and stopped to call Dakota back to the trail.

Near the top of the trail, the half cabin with an old potbellied stove looked lonely and abandoned. Through the evenings of Bethlehem Revisited, that pot-bellied stove warms the space while young Mary sits drop-spinning her wool. Gabriel finds her there and startles her with his message; and the visiting group shares in the good news.

Entering into the clearing, we soon pass the old rustic Bascom cabin, now known as Mary and Joseph's home. Here the Roman soldier on his trusty steed brings the news of a census.

At this point on our walk, Donk became interested in the grass in the clearing, but I kept him moving. We passed the gate to Bethlehem, the village, the stalls made of rough-sawn cedar planks and ramshackle boards. We skipped the trail that leads through the village to the storage shed, the full inn for those nights in December.

We crossed the lower pasture and headed to the top pasture. Up there we settled into a routine. Donk gave up trying to graze along the way and instead obediently walked beside me, moving his ears strategically to hear the various sounds, occasionally stopping, his ears pointed forward. He was intently watching something in the distance that I could not see or hear.

Dakota ran through the tall grass sniffing the ground, disappearing intermittently, then reappearing to check on Donk and me. We were all acting out our given natures. Dakota was being a dog, Donk was being a donkey, and I was doing the human thing: reminiscing. I recalled all the years I have walked, prayed, led students, and pointed others to this trail.

The trail hadn't always been here. In the early years, I'd forge my way through the blue-stem prairie on my daily prayer walks. Then Judd mowed a three-quarter mile path around the pasture for me. Once, when it grew over, and Judd was busy, I dragged the push mower up the rocky drive and mowed the path myself. Only once! I have more vision than brawn, and somehow I never had enough "vision" to do it again. Now, with riding mowers and tractor mowers, it seems there is always someone with enough vision to mow them when they begin to grow over. The trail is now a mainstay that serves many of us as a place to get away, to exercise, to walk and pray.

Dakota, Donk, and I had traversed the three-quarter-mile trail and were ready to head back down into the lower pasture. At the angel shelter I stopped to pick up a shiny, tin-foil angel halo apparently lost in the dark. The cedar-chipped outcrop where the angels stood was worn and compacted. Their short "Hallelujah Chorus" followed by "Joy to the World" seemed to echo softly across the valley. Leaving the upper pasture, we picked our way over the rocky path and headed toward the shepherd's fire pit and sheep pen, to the lower pasture. Stopping a moment, I once again found myself in reverie.

Memories. A few weeks ago, over two-thousand pairs of feet had tramped this path. I imagined I could hear the singers as they followed the groups caroling across the pasture. A few feet down the rocky path, Donk, Dakota and I passed the stump behind the cedar blind where "Gabriel" would sit, waiting for his cue.

Donk had carefully maneuvered the rocks, and Dakota, once she determined the direction we were heading, ran past us once again, leading the way. Passing the rustic sheep enclosure and rock-built fire pit, we continued toward the camels-and-wiseman iron silhouettes standing partially hidden in the little cedar alcove. Ashes filled the fire pit, and I remembered how strikingly poignant is the narrator's delivery he makes every year as he describes the stars, the excitement, and the miracle of the star that the long-ago wisemen followed.

As my animal friends and I continued down the trail, I saw, through the cedar trees, the outline of the barn. No children were running up the trail and shouting, "He is here! He is here! Come and see!" But I imagined I heard a faint echo. Oh, the wonder of memories!

Awe accompanied my gratitude. All this farm, community life, and ministry was a cloudy, quite unspecific dream those many years ago, and look what God wrought!

Did we have a master plan, in those early years, that we followed step-by-step? No! We faced many disappointments, incredible amounts of "just wait" times. Strategic people came and went. What was permanent was the land and God—and our faith that the Lord could take "what we held in our hands" and use it for his glory (see Exodus 4:2). And this, in turn, became our blessing!

My heart filled with gratitude. "It is God who works in you both to will and to do of his good pleasure." His pleasure was my blessing.

My walking companions that day had no recollections and

reminiscences. They simply found pleasure in "being." Donk was content being a donkey, and Dakota found joy in being a dog. But I have the opportunity to feed my eternal soul on what was, and is, and is to come. And I am in awe.

EPILOG
Markers of Blessing for New Stories

Dear Reader, you have traveled with me through my years of searching for the sacred. You have read my story of what God has done here on Kitten Creek Road. Now, I beg you, don't put this book down and forget that God is writing a story in *your* life also. After reading my story, don't miss your own!

As you listen to the noises of your city, your town, the busy highway that runs past your home, or sit in isolation down a lonely country road, do you yearn to find the joy of watching God unfold *your* story? Do you long for a community with which you can share life and experience mission? May I encourage you in your quest? The adventure is there waiting for you to discover, because God is there. You can step into that adventure wherever you are.

A few years ago, I found myself between new "book covers," trying to live out a new story. After thirty years in the old farmhouse, Judd and I moved into a new house our family built for us. Although we only moved a stone's throw across the road from the old farmhouse, we both faced the task of finding a new identity.

The first few weeks of living in a brand-new house felt

strange and foreign. I love *old*. I love the history of a house that has withstood many decades of occupation, one that has seen years of teeming life within its walls. Here I was in a house that had no history, and I remembered the Edgar Albert Guest poem that I had memorized during my young adult life: "It takes a heap o' livin' in a house to make it home."

By this time, much of my "livin'" had been in that cottage across the road. This new place held no memories and no vision. I was newly-retired and starting over again. I no longer could welcome someone to my farm and say, "Go out and walk the paths," nor plan a conference in the old barn.

Sara and Dan, my daughter and son-in-law, and their two boys are the caretakers and dreamers on that land now. And although our hearts are blessed to see the wonderful things they are doing, Judd and I must find our new particular path of ministry. How will we do that?

I have revisited the path I walked for many years. What were the markers along the way that made my journey so blessed? What disciplines, what habits, what attitudes kept me focused and enthusiastic?

The following trail markers are ones that I find myself reestablishing in my new story. Perhaps you, my friends, can also find encouragement from the following list. I am using this list, myself, to keep pointing me forward and upward.

MARKER #1:
Meet with God every day.

Come with a heart of expectation knowing that he is there, he loves you, and he wants to interact with you. Always have your Bible and your journal. I have found that my journal helps to make the thoughts in my heart more concrete. Listen to him. Respond with your whole being to what God is saying. Talk openly with him. He knows your heart; he created you and has walked with you from infancy, even when you did not know he was there.

MARKER #2:
Learn from mentors.

God's Spirit indwells the body of Christ. I have learned from others what grace looks like, how to love with unconditional love, how to open my heart to strangers, how to live a disciplined life, and so much more. They have been flesh and blood examples to me, yet that body of Christ includes those who may not have been our contemporaries or those who did not live in our geographic location. The authors I have read became my friends and challenged me to reach higher and delve deeper (see the Appendix for a list of these authors and their books).

MARKER #3:
Open your heart to others.

God can use every person who steps into your life. Each one is a gift. Some will add joy to your life. Some will bring challenges. But there will be no "mere mortals." In Henry J.M. Nouwen's 1975 book, *Reaching Out*, one chapter in particular left an imprint on my life: "From Hostility to Hospitality." In that chapter, he reminds the reader that "when our heart is filled with prejudices, worries, jealousies, there is little room for a stranger." Our hearts must be open and receptive to the gift the guest has to offer which is himself/herself, a person created in the image of God.

MARKER #4:

Use what God has placed in your hand.

Everything that you have has been a gift from God: your history, your family, your home, your money, your time. These gifts have been placed in your hand to use. You may hold tightly to them and desire to control them; or you may dismiss them as trivial or unimportant. But I have found if you release those gifts back to God, he can make them into an eternal product, something that will have everlasting value. Celebrate and be thankful for "every good and perfect gift that comes from the Father" (James 1:17).

MARKER #5:

Hold your plans and your dreams in an open hand.

How often the message of the world controls our choices. "You can achieve whatever you set as a goal." Society tells us that control of our lives is necessary. We feel like failures when we can't direct our lives and plans. God has better plans than our finite minds could ever dream. To develop plans, and to organize, is not wrong. But all those plans and activities must be constantly held out to God who may change them drastically. However, be content to know that his plans will be so much better than yours.

MARKER #6:

Be genuine.

Any time we try to take on someone else's gifts or persona, we are rejecting the person and the gifts intended for us. Any time we fake or hide our pain, our desires, our inadequacies, we are hiding from others and holding people at arm's length. Being genuine, being vulnerable, and being transparent will welcome others into your life and will allow God to use you in greater depth in other's lives.

MARKER #7:

Remember: your audience is God, and your readers are those who will observe your life.

You may never write a book; God will write it for you in your daily walk with him. And you will have achieved his applause. That is all you need.

APPENDIX

My Recommended-Reading List

These books and authors influenced my life greatly, becoming my friends and mentors. Newer writers and their work you may discover; but don't forget the old ones. C.S. Lewis recommended that for every new book one reads, an old classic should be read to avoid "chronological snobbery." I recommend these classics:

1. Books by Leanne Payne ... especially the following:
   The Real Presence; The Healing Presence; and *Listening Prayer.*

2. Books by Dallas Willard:
   In Search of Guidance (re-published by Intervarsity Press under the title, *Hearing God: Developing a Conversational Relationship with God*; *The Divine Conspiracy*; and *Renovation of the Heart.*

3. Books by C.S. Lewis ... all of his books, especially:
   Fiction: *Till We Have Faces; Perelandra; Screwtape Letters;* and *The Great Divorce.*
   Nonfiction: *The Problem of Pain; Mere Christianity;* and *The Weight of Glory.*

4. Books by the Schaeffers:
   L'Abri; Hidden Art of Homemaking; The Tapestry; and *What is a Family?* by Edith Schaeffer
   He is There and He is Not Silent; How Shall We Then Live?; No Little People; etc. by Francis Schaeffer.

5. Books by others:

St. Benedict's Toolbox: The Nuts and Bolts of Everyday Benedictine Living by Jane Tomaine

The Sacred Romance: Drawing Closer to the Heart of God by Brent Curtis and John Eldredge

Poustinia by Catherine Doherty

The *Mitford* novels by Jan Karon

God's Passion for His Glory by John Piper

ABOUT THE AUTHOR

Nancy Swihart has served as Professor of English and Department Head of General Studies at Manhattan Christian College; editor and writer for National Center for Fathering; speaker at various women's retreats and conferences; and founding member of Wellspring, Inc. She co-authored the book, *Beside Every Great Dad* (Tyndale, 1993). Nancy and her husband, Jud, a counselor, have three grown children and eleven grandchildren.

Retired now, the Swiharts are enjoying a time of reflection, a time of volunteering and serving, and a time of stretching to meet the new challenges of ordering their days that they may present to the Lord hearts of wisdom.

Follow Nancy and her reflections from the farm at http://www.nancyswihart.com/.

CPSIA information can be obtained
at www.ICGtesting.com
Printed in the USA
FFOW04n0705190517
35735FF